SEMMELWEIS

BY THE SAME AUTHOR

The Mediterranean Runs Through Brooklyn

Valentino and the Great Italians

Conversation with Johnny

BART: A Life of A. Bartlett Giamatti

Anita Garibaldi, a Biography

The Little Sailor, a Romantic Thriller

Toni Cade Bambara's One Sicilian Night, a memoir

John Dante's Inferno, a Playboy's Life

Dante in Love

IMMIGRANTS, according to Anthony Valerio
(vols. 1 & 2)

iv

semmelweis,

LIFE & WORK OF IGNAZ P. SEMMELWEIS☐

Drawings of Semmelweis young and ill by
permission of the artist. Acrylic mixed media on
canvas painting©Aharon Gluska2019.
Cover design & images of hand washings & collage
by permission of the artist. ©Dave Barry2019.

ISBN: 978-0-9904675-5-7

Library of Congress Control Number: 2020906884

About SEMMELWEIS

In a global #metoo moment, Semmelweis should also have his place as someone who listened to women and, significantly, to their ailing bodies, even as the medical profession dismissed a common affliction killing women as a "woman's illness" and therefore not worthy of a place on the forefront of medicine. There is a photo circling the internet of the actor Patrick Stewart holding a sign with the Amnesty International seal. The caption for this image, presumably in Stewart's own words, is this: "People won't take you seriously unless you're an old white man, and since I'm an old white man I'm going to use that to help the people who need it." The sign Stewart is holding reads: Defend right for girls and women. Semmelweis, like Stewart, believed in embodied response, of putting one's body behind and into one's words. To be sure, Semmelweis was a pioneering physician and scientist whose accomplishments should be studied for their contributions to science. But he was also a feminist, and his work should be understood in that vein, also.--**Ellen Nerenberg, Hollis Professor of Romance Languages & Literatures, Wesleyan University**

On a school outing with my 9- and 10-year-old classmates to the local cinema we saw a film about the life and work of Dr. Semmelweis. I knew about him from school but even more from my parents; at home I read about famous Hungarian heroes, not just kings and warriors, but those ignored in their lifetime, whose work could have benefited all, children, women, and men. Our history, so full of tragedies like his, unrealized potential: failed reformers and inventors, scientists and artists embittered and ignored, driven to early death. –**Akös Őstor, professor, author, filmmaker**

Anthony Valerio has written an eye-opening, riveting, and truly feminist book about a champion of suffering women, Dr. Semmelweis. It is heartbreaking to read of the enormous number of young women who died of childbed fever due to the unsanitary practices in hospitals of the 19th century. Semmelweis predated the discovery of germs as the source of infections, but he intuited the connection between unhealthy, dirty materials and the deaths of young mothers exposed to them through the unwashed hands of their examining doctors. So simple! Wash your hands! But, as Valerio vividly recounts, the resistance to Semmelweis's discovery was enormous and fairly unrelenting, due in great part to the sheer arrogance of Alpha male doctors. I read this powerful book in one sitting, and came away with great admiration for both its author and its subject. Thank you, Anthony Valerio, for shining light on a still too obscure hero, and thank you, Dr. Semmelweis, for your devotion to easing the suffering of women, and for honoring mothers, the givers of life. Read this book, men and women alike. It is one of Valerio's best.—Rebecca West, emeritus, University of Chicago

Looking at and understanding someone like Semmelweis on a deep level and how he combated prejudices and prevailing thoughts and changed the way medicine is practiced is as relevant today as it was in the 1840s.—
Prakash Sampath, M.D. Surgeon. President, Rhode Island Neurological Institute

For:

...the Hungarian physician Ignaz Philipp Semmelweis, the physician who discovered the causes of that horrible scourge called childbed, or puerperal, fever, and its means of prevention. Largely ignored and, at the same time knowing that his program of prophylaxis was saving life upon life of new mothers around the world, as well as their babies, he was driven mad, infected himself with a surgical knife, was committed to a public insane asylum, where, in an attempt to escape, was thrown to the ground and, lying helpless, was bludgeoned to death.

...friend and colleague the great American author Kurt Vonnegut, who requested of me a rare book entitled *Semmelweis,* by Dr. Louis Ferdinand Destouches,* written for his Thesis in Medicine in Paris, 1924. Following Kurt Vonnegut's accidental, ridiculous death as a result of a fall on his front stoop, when he had told me in all soberness that he was suing the tobacco company because he'd been a chain Pall Mall smoker for many decades and, at the age of 84, had still not contracted cancer, I wondered why Kurt was fascinated by the life of Semmelweis. Here was, at least on the surface for which he was famous, a science fiction writer, transforming Earth time and places and human beings to other worldly creatures and planets, while Semmelweis devoted his life to preserving human life at its very inception on planet Earth. Semmelweis claimed that "decaying organic animal matter" [later called "germs"] was the leading cause of childbed fever. Maybe Vonnegut had this in mind, employing human decay for something better--for research, progress, just as Semmelweis held.

...Dr. Elizabeth C. Jones, a pediatrician who answered my questions generously and who, near and far, in Samoa and Hawaii, New Orleans,

Chicago and Florida, cared for thousands of healthy children in nuclear households and also those children who managed to survive and were raised in orphanages. In the time of Semmelweis, babies who survived their deceased mothers were placed in foundling homes, which Semmelweis could see outside his hospital window. Semmelweis forces us to explore our deepest regions, our births. I asked Dr. Jones about her experience with children in orphanages. She told me: "Many children left in such situations developed what was called 'Hospitalism'. They became depressed, unresponsive, catatonic. This was first described in England but I forget the doctor's name [possibly, Alexander Gordon]. Of course, with large numbers of children, there were always numerous diseases that would sweep through these places: measles, meningitis, typhoid, etc. Many would die. Some acquired sequelie: blindness, cerebral palsy, etc.

TABLE OF CONTENTS

"...there is no discovery in the whole history of medicine that, by protecting against a disease, can save as many human lives as my teaching regarding protection against childbed fever."—Dr. Ignaz P. Semmelweis

"The laws of nature are the same throughout the world."—Dr. Ignaz Semmelweis

"puerperal"*—derived from puer, Latin for child, meaning to bring forth."—Edward Strother, A Critical Essay on Fevers, 1716.

Author's Note

The last draft of this book was written in 2019, a year before the present pandemic of Coronavirus.

"Semmelweis," utters the nurse.

It is more than 170 years since the time of Dr. Ignaz P. Semmelweis, not in his imperial hospital in Vienna but here in St. Joseph's of Connecticut, U.S.A., and not in one of his lying-in clinics but in a post-op recovery orthopedic ward. Thankfully have regained consciousness and raise up on elbows to see once again the immediate world. Fix immediately on a hand sanitizer, physicians and staff passing and wetting their hands almost mechanically. Several more such sanitizers are strewn around the ward, I observe.

"So many," I say, to no one in particular.

But my nurse, though staring into her computer screen, reading my vitals, hears. It is now that she says,

"Semmelweis."

Why, Semmelweis? Why embark on the journey through his life and work today? Quixotic from the onset because in this the 21st century the one superseding, overriding phenomenon culled from Semmelweis for this writer is the power and everlasting potential of the power of observation. Seeing, feeling, coalescing, harnessing natural unadorned phenomena for the benefit of mankind….Blind poet Homer could have cured cancer as well as, say, an all-observing man or woman on the planet Earth today or in the future.

The doctor himself said that the laws of nature are the same throughout the world and, if this were true then perhaps it is also true now and some physician, some researcher, even some botanist is capable of observing one of these laws gone awry and then set it right and cure H.I.V., cancer. Or observe same in a plant and find such cures. Today, planet Earth is under siege by the hands of its inhabitants. I can picture Kurt Vonnegut shaking his head in agreement and displeasure—especially at some heads of state—so is such a cure even possible through once natural laws?

Vonnegut states that the life of Semmelweis is a "beneficial example for all mankind." Am I writing on an example in some expansive way? The ways Semmelweis, through his work, benefitted all mankind? The countless lives he saved through hand washings and the surgical nail brush he invented. A listing of ways….?

In his great book *Slaughterhouse 5*, celebrating its 50th year this year—the author states that on the planet Tralfalmadore, "…when a person dies, he is still very much alive in the past, so it is very silly to cry at his funeral. All moments, past, present and future always have existed, always will exist."

4

On the dying planet Earth, Semmelweis lives.

In response to any meaning Semmelweis might have today, Hungarian scholar/author/filmmaker Ákos Őstör says:

"Denial in the face of empirical evidence: how contemporary is that."

A nurse…. There were 140 nurses in Semmelweis's hospital, a mixture of lay and Catholic, wearing long uniforms of dark-blue flannel bellowed by underlying petticoats, starched white apron covering from breast to ankles, fluffy linen cap tied under the chin. Portrayed as kind and caring, two such nurses greet the mostly young, single pregnant women nearing term after they knock on the imperial hospital's great white door. They have made their way through the hospital's maze of many enclosed buildings, walkways and inner courtyards. It takes a good few hours to get through it all, as it is the largest and most famous hospital in the world. A fitting locale for their newborns. Smiling, two nurses one on each arm, the expectant mother climbs a steep staircase at the top of which is a small, wooden table. A bearded young man sits, notebook open in front of him. He looks up. Attempts a smile. It is Assistant Dr. Ignaz P. Semmelweis, Clerk of Records.

He is at the outset of his career, 28 years old, of medium height, stocky, with a full black beard and head of hair already with receding hairline. His forehead is wide and endless, and his mustache is in the shape of a pair of lips. His eyes are all-seeing, with thin, arching brows, the left turned up slightly. His lips are also thin, and relaxed. A sharp nose with flaring nostrils.

I have attempted to present his life and work through his eyes, mind and heart. At the same time, experience as deeply as possible the horror of a new mother who contracted childbed fever in the days immediately after giving the gift of life. Her motherhood denied. Sudden farewell to her newborn. Attempting in a flash to see how he or she will turn out. Identifying with her pain, the pity. Unimaginable pain, for the post-partum "twilight sleep" of a combination of morphine and scopolamine, an amnesiac, would not be introduced until 60-odd years later. To comprehend the life of Ignaz Semmelweis, one must also plumb oneself, we children who survived.

A word about his name. His parents named him Ignác Fülöp. Since this document is written originally in English, which language in all its beauty hopefully brings the good doctor's life and work to light, I have taken the liberty for which I ask his forgiveness to translate his given name here to Ignaz Philipp.

It is more difficult to honor the memory of the nameless than that of the known.--Walter Benjamin*

The victims of childbed fever--that is, all of Semmelweis's patients--were, of course, women. Anonymous women all. Pregnant women who had stood before the Clerk of Records in order to be placed in one or the other of the lying-in clinics. Women he examined and delivered, the majority successfully. The facilitators of their individual tragedies, thousands in his time around the world-- whom, toward the end of his life, Semmelweis called "murderers"--for they would not use his hand- washings of a solution of chloride of lime—were, for the most part, all men. Even some midwives*, early in his career, were men. And the good, caring nurses who, day in and day out, night after night, heard the foreboding sound of the priest's bell that preceded him come to administer Last Rites, who witnessed the anguish of a new mother about to lose her life, they, too, were capable of transferring the disease through the contaminated animal matter on their unwashed hands.

Men can only imagine, often witness, the wondrous act of a woman giving birth. Dr. L.F. Destouches, a.k.a. Céline, wrote that the pain a woman endures in childbirth is commensurate to the pain a man experiences in cardiac infarct. A man has to suffer the pain and anguish of a major heart attack to approximate what a woman feels during the process of childbirth. Regarding a new mother in the throes of childbed fever, Dr. Elizabeth Jones says:

"The literary descriptions are probably correct, even worse."

In his cornerstone book *The Doctor's Plague,* surgeon/author Sherwin B. Nuland* attempts such a literary description. Dr. Nuland follows a woman through the cycle of conception and term of pregnancy and stages of her affliction, accompanied up to a point by her parents, and then, like a prizefighter once the bell sounds, everyone leaves and she alone partakes alone of the miracle of birth. Horror commences with looking into the face of her newborn and feeling, hearing, smelling and kissing her baby but then he/she has to be taken away because late in the afternoon of giving birth, the new mother who has contracted the Fever begins to feel "…increasing discomfort in her lower abdomen…she was unable to eat her supper of thin soup and potato…her fingers touching her abdomen worsened her pain…a blue color under the icy fingernails…" Suddenly, out of the cruel night, a bell tolls. It's that of the priest who has come to administer Last Rites. The sacristan rings the viaticum rhythmically. All of the women, healthy as well as ill, new mothers as well as expectant, know exactly what this tolling portends. It is the death knell. It announces that another new mother is about to die. At first, the bell sounds faint, then it approaches--closer…closer…louder…louder. The breaths of the women quicken...Countless times Semmelweis would stare down upon such a young mother's eyes reflecting unimaginable pain, beyond words, her face flushed, livid color fixed in the cheeks, skin hot and dry, pulse quick and weak, shortness of breath that reflected fear and dread of making a full inspiration, of dilating the thorax. Dr. Nuland continues: "...three days after her baby's birth—the girl suddenly sat bolt upright in her bed, her eyes staring wildly forward. With arms outstretched...and fell back on the pillow, dead."

The priest, the bell that preceded him silenced for the time being, administers Last Rites:

"Through this holy anointing, and by His most tender mercy, may the Lord pardon you what sins you have committed...."

A few words about a literary device involving tense and time. After living and working on this project for two years, the time of Semmelweis's historic tenure in Vienna, he emerges so real, so much a contemporary, so alive at any given moment, as are the feelings of the mostly young, disenfranchised pregnant women he sought to save that, instead of stating this, a switch is made to the present tense.

I have taken painstaking care that the scientific material presented is accurate and factual. Along with facts I have tried to glimpse the good doctor's heart.

Semmelweis managed to write, "Early on I developed an innate aversion to anything which can be called writing."

Maybe his life would have been a little easier if he had published his findings around the time of their discovery, according to precedent. He read avidly, alone, late at night, by gaslight. About childbed fever and he read the books of his great teachers and the pioneering physicians who had preceded him. He knew he had to write up his findings but could not. The voice of this writing reflects the pain Semmelweis suffered to do so himself, ten years too late, which caused him great harm, for now his detractors could say that he had failed to verify his findings through published papers and books.

With hand washings of his solution of chloride of lime, the rate of death from childbed fever plummeted from unspeakable levels, upwards of double digits to 1.3 %.

If it were left for Semmelweis to summarize his work in written words, he might do so with only five:

My Results Speak For Themselves.

Lastly, the hope is that today, around the world, at this moment, when one is passing surely one of millions of hand sanitizers and uses it to cleanse the hands, a thought can possibly go out to

Dr. Ignaz Semmelweis and a fuller understanding, and appreciation, of his life and work.

Anthony Valerio – 20/20

PART I: HOME

His mother wrote…that she worried about her son's' "impetuous nature." And he had "difficulty with language."

Budapest's Tában park is surrounded by baroque villas and majestic apartments of a century before. The thermal baths that resemble the ancient hammams of Istanbul are still here. The dark, gated group of houses of prostitution has been transformed to guest houses. His first home, located at Meindle-Haus, today 1-3 Apròd Street, used to stand in the shadow of St. Stephen's church and, in this home in shadow, on the first day of July 1818, Terézia Müller Semmelweis gave life to her fifth child, whom she and her husband named Ignác Fülöp.

He was born also into a world dominated by the Congress of Vienna (November 1814-June 1815). It amounted to the adage, To the Victor Belong the Spoils. The defeat of Napoleon I established Austria as the iron-fist ruler of most of Europe, with Prince Klemens Wenzel von Metternich dictator. Former reactionary practices were restored. Jews and Liberals were once again herded into ghettoes and could not convene nor speak to one another. The Jesuit order was restored. Taxes were raised. Civil reforms such as freedom of speech and assembly were repealed. Hungary, as well as Italy, was carved up like so many leaves of an artichoke, and a puppet pope was elected in Rome. In Vienna's great Imperial General Hospital, a conservative Education Minister appointed physicians, and senior professors such as Johann Klein wielded powerful influence at court.

Terézia Müller Semmelweis was the daughter of a prosperous coach manufacturer and so was accustomed to the finer things in life. She was also, it's said, "a hard-working woman, married young, pretty, too, indefatigable…."--Dr. L.F. Destouches

Which, by necessity, tending to the rearing and needs of nine children, fatigue, at least exhibiting it, was not an option.

The cries of nine babies….Her constitution had to have been extremely strong in order to endure nine pregnancies, all successfully. She was fertile, just like Empress Maria Theresa. Then she undertook the indefatigable work of attending to the unforgiving needs of nine children. Clean, shop, cook, watch over—is it that much different today?

Of her many children, what did Terézia Müller notice about her son Ignác that would qualify him by outstanding men to be a "genius"?

She knew when he was unhappy. Once, she wrote to Semmelweis's major mentor Dr. Joseph Skoda* in Vienna that she worried about her son's' "impetuous nature." And he had "difficulty with language."

The fifth of nine children, Ignaz's position was a kind of fulcrum: four siblings had come before him and four would come after. Semmelweis was also the fulcrum of old and new ideas in medicine.

And the fulcrum of old and new systems of government.

Maybe one reason Ignác grew to be a restless, incredibly persistent and stubborn young man who did not suffer fools gladly and often waxed sarcastic, and who had to fight relentlessly for what he wanted, was because he was born into a bevy of other children, with their chorus of needs and pleads and plays. He was born into a situation in which you could not be spoiled. You listened, behaved. Did what your father instructed, at least at first. He grew in the midst of a healthy, fertile, hard-working mother, successful father and normal, healthy brothers and sister.

His father, József Semmelweis, was a successful merchant with his own wholesale spice and general consumer goods shop. He was prominent, holding the position of *Obervorsteher,*

Chairman of the Grocers' Association. His store, part of his house, had a sign outside: *Weißen Elefanten,* at the White Elephant. From a photograph of the period, he looks like a shrewd, robust businessman. The name Semmelweis suggests that he was Jewish. For the legions of enemies Ignaz Semmelweis would attract to himself, the fact that his name sounded Jewish was quite enough. Had not Empress Maria Theresa herself proclaimed forty years before Semmelweis was born:

"I know of no greater plague than this race, which on account of its deceit, usury and avarice is driving my subjects into vagary. Therefore, as far as possible, the Jews are to be kept away and avoided."

Dr. Semmelweis refused to be kept away. He made himself unavoidable.

At the same time, the quarter century of French Wars (1792-1815) provided Jewish entrepreneurs with excellent economic opportunities. Wholesale merchants, who were predominantly Jewish, supplied the army with goods, and József Semmelweis had strong connections with the army of King Franz. Even the royal household needed a continual supply of paprika and caviar.

The Semmelweis house, built in the Gothic style, was a happy one, filled with shouting, singing and dancing. There was much grinding of dried peppers and paprika. Rich aromas permeated the house.

Born into a well-to-do family, later on in his capacity of Clerk of Records he was able to recognize the opposite, hardship and strife, and empathize with the mainly single pregnant teenagers who came to his clinic from the "comfortless classes."

Joy. He knew what joy was. Sorrow. He could recognize sorrow.

His first mix of languages was the German dialect of his father and other merchants, called Buda-Swabian, and the German of his mother, who was from Bavaria. He grew up speaking a decidedly regional Hungarian. But did not all human beings whatever their origin, language and beliefs, for thousands of years and forever, possess two ears and eyes and one nose and mouth, and organs and functions more or less the same? And as he'd already learned at home, had we not, all of us, every single one, from the beginning of time to the most recent moment, come from a woman?

"Chance is the street. The street changing and multiplying truths to infinity, simpler than books."—Dr. L.F. Destouches

And then Ignaz bounded onto the narrow, hillside, cobbled streets. Look up. The sky's immensity, its grandeur. Listen...St. Steven's organ. Closer, closer.... It pervades your deepest regions.

Pass the restaurants, bars—tinkling silver/glass ware…drifting aroma of beer. The bordellos are quiet, in shadow. His town was called a Bohemian town. Tourists came also for the wine. He would have been right at home in Greenwich Village, Haight Ashbury, Hamburg. There is something wonderful about chance. Nature itself is governed by chance. One never knows. Unpredictable is the appearance of someone, some thing not encountered before. Fleeting yet always fresh, always new. In the game of cops and robbers, there's always a new victor, always a new victim. Throwing or kicking his ball—always a different trajectory and destination, boy or girl on the receiving end. What is the relationship between the idea of chance and Semmelweis's early affinity to street life and his work in medicine, specifically obstetrics? The highly unlikely joining of a sperm cell and an egg? Become the equally unlikely guardian to assure that nature's way follows a path of normalcy in regards to the woman's spectacular human body and that new life ensues in a healthy way? Observe. Around lunchtime, the streets teem with musicians. Citizens of the world. Travel at their own expense to new cities, new audiences. Ignác took away from home his love of singing and dancing. He joined in the chorus. You could sing a Gypsy folk song a thousand times and it was always fresh. Or jump and kick your heels or clack your spoon for years on end. There's the musician with his guitar of four loose strings. He would appear after a heavy rain, in threadbare clothes, looking around with a sullen face. The boy stands on a dry patch of cobbles amid puddles. If he decides to approach, he has to stand and listen with dry shoes. The musician scratches himself and swallows hard, imagining the lunch passersby will soon have. A few stop. The boy watches from against the far wall because he's shorter than everyone else. Dr. Destouches breathes life into the scene:

"From a piss-stained bag the musician pulls out a guitar with loose strings...The thing sobs beneath his dirty fingers...He looks skyward, the wind...With his sickly voice he throws out a few searching sounds, a few of us stop, and others with us...just as little Philipp did once. A circle forms and grows, crowding the pavement, getting in the way of passing carriages. A magic circle...this wretch with his scratchy notes wants to lead us from our lives...and with what? ...Let's follow him...A little way into his Dream."

O *tempora, o mores!* Shame on the age and on its principles!--Cicero, *in Catilinam*

A little way into his Dream he begins formal schooling. What a torment. His brothers József and Fülűp preceded him to Gymnasiun--therefore, he had to attend. He proved to be an industrious, able student. No one had the slightest idea what he was feeling and thinking. His difficulties with language his mother alluded to include lessons in the first language of his country, Hungarian, as well as the more deep-rooted Magyar, which would interest Semmelweis later on during and after the time of the revolution of 1848. His lessons were subsumed to the teaching of German and Latin. Textbook German did not improve upon his dialect of German, and he hated Latin. Still, he managed to graduate Gymnasium with second-level honors, barely able to speak his country's native language.

And he had not the slightest idea about what he wanted to do. But his father knew. József Semmelweis had a spectacular future mapped out for his fifth child. The boy is level-headedness, has a facility with numbers, an eye for accuracy and details and a love of the outdoors. A Royal Auditor, that's what Ignaz will become. Supplying Emperor Franz's court with spices and caviar will open the way for the young man to become such a royal clerk for the emperor's vast, powerful army. The position was filled with judges on horseback. And so this son would have a horse of his own and on his horse ride around and arbitrate disputes between troops in the field and cheated, angry landowners. Buda was a free, royal city, was it not? So, such disputes were settled without violence and bloodshed. Like the bourgeois family that they were, Ignác Philipp would become a successful, respected judge and marry and have a family of his own.

Walk beside young Semmelweis carrying a bundle under his arm across the long, wooden, noble bridge that spans the Danube. In a few years, he will cross a modern bridge, that of the Chain Bridge connecting Buda and Pest, the west and east sides of Budapest. Look yonder at your interminable river Danube, how it passes through five countries where you have never been and into which your work will penetrate. Down at the ships carrying merchandise of trade from distant parts to your father's shop, then back out again. Up at the immense sky over the world. That Latin again. Follows like a hulking shadow. How it galls. And Cicero with his damn lists.

Later on, he would create his own lists of the myriad ways women came into harm's way at the hands of men. His own list of the ways men could prevent the scourge of childbed fever and did not. But now he was on his way to Pest Academy, according to his father's prescription. A high school preparatory program that paved the undesired way to the University of Vienna and the study of law.

Prize lists do not include his name. At the same time, he grew to love his city, its gardens, its promenades.

Away from his parents' scrutiny and his teachers, just he and good friend Lajos Markusovszky, they could steal into a house of prostitution and not account for the hour of pleasure. And every Sunday he walk backed across the bridge for dinner at home.

A typical Sunday repast consisted of a hearty soup, beef stew, spicy casserole, cake and pastries. The kitchen was warm with onions braising in hot lard. The aroma of paprika still pervades.

No matter how many Sundays you go home for a visit and dinner, the bridge you came in on leads you, inexorably, out to your future.

Ignaz Philipp managed to graduate from high school in November 1837.

In the freezing cold of 4 November 1837, at the precise age of 19 years 3 months and 18 days, Ignaz Philipp Semmelweis set out from his native city of Buda for the capital city of Vienna.

Wearing a black kimono with three quarter sleeves, he bobs up and down to the beat of the coach and four. Maybe this fine coach was provided by his wealthy Bavarian maternal grandfather, at the least a sturdy one. Rambling through Pressburg in the northeast, on the Danube's left bank, its castle up there reduced to rubble by Napoleon I's fleeting victory. Skirt the base of the Little Carpathian Mountain's outlying spurs. Ordinarily, the journey from Buda to Vienna took four days but with Semmelweis nothing was ordinary. Two border gendarmes block the road. One takes the reins, the other approaches his compartment.

Travel documents in order?

Semmelweis reaches into his coat, withdraws his passport and hands in through the open window.

One gendarme turns to his fellow. "...this one's a hick..."

But no matter the spoken and written language, did not all human beings whatever their origin, language and beliefs, for thousands of years and forever, possess two ears and eyes and one nose and mouth, and organs and functions more or less the same?

The gendarmes slap a rump and off we fly.

PART II: VIENNA

In Vienna, he grew to love each and every anonymous new mother whose life was spared due to his program of prophylaxis. A singularly private moment, hidden from history.—A.V.

Young Semmelweis, graphite pencil, Aharon
Gluska, 2019

Upon his first spoken words in the capital city of Vienna, announcing his name to the registrar, say, he was taken for a Jew with a small-town accent.

His new home consisting of the general hospital/law and medical schools complex called *Allgemeine Krankenhaus* had eight courtyards, a maze of 111 rooms, 500 beds including one for him, two lying-in clinics--which he will come to know extremely well--its own asylum and a foundling hospital for newborns whose mothers die of childbed fever. Large entranceway made of wood. He walks through...

Obtain a degree in the law then, through his father's connections, the Austrian court will appoint him judge and he will ride horses and mediate disputes between the military and angry landowners. The very thought weighs on his strong shoulders.

He writes to Lajos back in Buda:

"How I miss our city, our gardens, our promenades. Nothing pleases me here."

His unhappiness over the study of Austrian law may have merged with his alien surroundings, at least those he visited. The legality of houses of prostitution was an up and down affair. Licensed one year, outlawed the next. The year of his arrival happened to be an off year. Semmelweis himself did not offer detailed reasons for his unhappiness in the metropolis, but life would "formulate them for him in the near future, with the utmost precision," writes Dr. L.F.Destouches.

The more Semmelweis studied Austrian law, the more he understood that one day he would abandon it. Austria was Hungary's conqueror but not the legislator of his life's path. Law as a course of study was as predictable and stolid as Metternich's iron hand ruling it. It did not present an iota of mystery, of chance, of song. Despite the various cultures and languages and histories that made up the Austrian Empire—Poles, Hungarians, Italians, Czechs, Slovaks, Serbs, Croats, Dalmatians, Romanians—all were governed and regulated as if they were Austrian. And he could listen to the sound of his own voice speaking to a native Viennese and feel like a denizen from a distant planet. Worse, his courses required writing in formal German. But he hated writing...in any language. The transcribed products of the act of writing were simply too permanent, easily discovered as contradictory. Finally, he could not imagine himself some sort of judge governed by the exchange of words both spoken and written.

Like so many aspects of Semmelweis's life there were as many positives as the opposite. His aversion to the study of law guided him to a course of study with a language all its own, that of the human body and its makeup, of health and sickness, of human beings in pain. A course of study restricted, at that time, to the called few.

His great, tumultuous future was upon him.

It happened just like that, purely by happenstance. One ordinary day, a friend enrolled in medical school invited him to audit a lecture.

The friends walk down to the medical school cellar, the stairwell damp and stale, then they stand in a circle with medical students around a patient in bed suffering from a "fever," attended by Vienna's most renowned physician, Dr. Joseph Skoda.* Skoda percusses the patient's chest to feel and listen for pathological changes in the heart, lungs, and thoracic activity. Prevalent among the pandemics of the day that produced high fevers such as this one were cholera, yellow fever, influenza, puerperal fever, and typhus. One student asks about a therapy that could possibly attach to this fever. Skoda shrugs his shoulders.

"Ach, da ist ja alles eins!" "They're all the same!"

Skoda's sterling reputation has carried down to the present. Dr. Elizabeth Jones writes:

"Skoda is a great name in medicine. His anatomy book is a classic and much prized. It is a rare medical book."[*]

Joseph Skoda incorporated into his teaching and work the most current instruments and methods of diagnostics, including auscultation and percussion. When Semmelweis watched him on this first occasion, stethoscope around his neck, his ear ausculating, his finger palpitating, Skoda had already published a treatise entitled *Auscultation and Percussion.*

Semmelweis knew from the beginning that medical innovators had to publish their findings as a way of verifying them.

Here is an excerpt from this treatise which Semmelweis may have been listening to at that very moment:

38

"... with fever and disturbance of the respiratory system, it is certainly true that loud vesicular respiration occasionally pre-cedes the crepitating rale (an abnormal rattling sound heard when examining unhealthy lungs with a stethoscope). But this is no reason for setting up an especial first stage of pneumonia, this symptom being even less constant than crepitating rale. The signs...."

The sun rising on the next day after observing Dr. Joseph Skoda's examination of the fever victim witnesses a curious Semmelweis walking back down those hard, dank steps to the hospital basement. The room is cold, like the stairwell. A lay nurse was changing linen. She turns at the door.

"*Tot,*""dead," pointing up, not to heaven but to *Autopsie* on the third floor.

Somewhere, in a dream perhaps, he already knew. Ding! The priest's bell in the middle of the night, just outside his room, had announced it.

Then Semmelweis makes his way up, as much out of curiosity as by his knowledge that by government edict all patients who died had to be given an autopsy. Guided by the awful, unforgiving smell of putrefaction of decaying organic animal matter, he climbs slowly, deliberately. Closer, closer, that godforsaken odor....Enter a room that, at first, gives one to pause. It resembles a busy butcher shop. Blood all over. On the surgeon's hands, rolled up sleeves, forearms, shirt.

The professor performing the autopsy was Karl von Rokitansky,* Professor of Pathological Anatomy. No physician in the entire world of medicine from that day in the early 1840s to this one in 2019 bloodied his hands more than Rokitansky. Normally, autopsies were performed by the deceased's physician. Not so when Rokitansky became hospital director. He performed *all* autopsies—30,000 over his 40-year career: two per day, seven days a week.

"For the sake of consistency," the surgeon wrote. "Of seeing with my own eyes the deceased's affected organs, by way of seeking patterns, establishing categories of diseases, for the sake of clarification and clarity of distinct diseases."

Observing with his own eyes, the greatest of Rokitansky's teachings.

Looming over the cadaver, scalpel in bare hand, white shirt sleeves rolled up, black cravat in place, the great pathological surgeon makes a neat incision in the abdomen, resulting in a stench of putrid flesh combined with a burst of fetid fluid....

Still, despite the nature of his work, surrounded by so much disease and death, Rokitansky remained a congenial sort, the perfect antidote to his student Semmelweis's moody, irascible nature.

Semmelweis looks back at the pale lifeless face. No written words can describe what he sees, feels. A day or so before giving birth then a glean in that face of pride and happiness. Only last night down with Fever…

Dr. Semmelweis

Why, not how—that is the question.

There was little in Semmelweis's childhood to indicate that he would pursue a career in medicine. As we have seen, the eleven members of his family enjoyed good health, and he himself had been a hearty, healthy boy and young man. Medicine may have seemed a freer study than the law. The Congress of Vienna had not legislated the workings of the human body, of disease and cures and means of prevention thereof. Medicine seemed outside the realm of politics and the auspices of man-made laws, like the ones that governed disputes between the Prussian army and Austrian landowners. The human body was the natural state of things. The healthy human body fell sick, and there was no greater challenge, no greater calling, than to seek to heal it.

"Great works are those which awaken our genius. Great men are those who give them a form.--Dr. L.F. Destouches

In 1844, at the age of 26, Semmelweis, without informing his father, exchanged the study of law for the study of medicine. What a fortunate turn of events to have Dr. Joseph Skoda and Dr. Karl von Rokitansky as your first instructors. In addition to being cornerstones in the study and practice of internal medicine and surgery, what qualities did they possess that allowed Semmelweis to spring into himself, discover his talents, realize his potential? Skoda could be gruff, abrupt. Rokitansky, even tempered. Semmelweis appears to have possessed some of both. Certainly, they cared and advocated for him. Attempted, especially Skoda, to save

Semmelweis from his personal demons. Semmelweis himself inspired these great physicians to go beyond the classroom, bedsides and surgical theaters to the nature of their protégée, his genius, his discoveries. Finally, and perhaps most important, they understood the importance of his work for generations to come.

These were men and physicians who had deigned to enter the dark, virgin territory of disease and health amid periods of wars and repressive governments.

From Joseph Skoda he learned about the instruments and techniques developed by two great former colleagues: Leopold Aunbrügger (1722-1809) and Jean Corvisart* (1755-1821). Auenbrügger's story is fascinating. Born in Graz in Styria, an Austrian province, Auenbrügger's father was a well-to-do innkeeper who served spices that József Semmelweis sold in his shop. In the cool basement of this inn stood barrels of wine which fascinated little Leopold. One day, playing down there, the boy tapped a barrel--it made a sound. After some wine was taken from this barrel, Leopold tapped it again—it made a different sound. He tapped this same barrel a few times before any more wine was taken. This sound became familiar. It and it alone translated to the level of wine in the barrel now. As more and more wine was taken from this barrel, the sound his tap-tap tapping finger made changed. The different sound was the same when the next barrel had been freed of the exact amount of wine. Sounds depended on changing levels inside the barrels. Full barrels made one sound, barrels half-full another, and so forth. By the sound their percussing finger produced, Leopold and then his father could ascertain the various levels of wine in their barrels. How useful. Plan inventory, create a timetable of wine production. Leopold's father, like Semmelweis's, urged his son to study law at the

University of Vienna. The young man and his cultivated fingers and ears traveled with him, and soon he shifted his study from law to medicine. Glory be the common unheeded plans of fathers for their children. Auenbrügger worked and experimented on his patients alive and deceased for ten years in the Spanish Military Hospital. Fortunate it was for these pioneers of medicine—Skoda, Rokitansky and then Semmelweis, that they could dissect and learn from cadavers. As far back as the Renaissance in Italy, artists such as Leonardo Da Vinci and Michelangelo Buonarotti, in order to study human anatomy with some exactitude, had to steal into cemeteries at night and disinter bodies. Auenbrügger would place a heavy cloth over a patient's lungs, percuss and feel and hear a drum-like sound. He experimented on a real drum over which he had placed a cloth. A diseased lung with pneumonia, he found, sounded like the fleshy part of the thigh being tapped. He had to keep in mind the different sounds and be capable of describing them. Auenbrügger kept records of the sounds of organs and their differences. He experimented with soundings of the heart. Tapping the area over the heart produced a dull-like sound, so that, in this way, the limits of heart dullness, that is, a healthy heart, could be determined.

No instrument, no genius even could measure the magnanimity of the hearts of these great physicians.

Auenbrügger published his finding in a book entitled *Inventum Novum*. Or, in English, *A New Discovery that Enables the Physician from the Percussion of the Human Thorax to Detect the Diseases Hidden Within the Chest*. The book was largely ignored. Auenbrügger wrote:

"I have not been unconscious of the dangers I must encounter, since it has always been the fate of those who have illustrated or improved the arts and sciences by their discovery, to be beset by envy, malice, hatred, detraction, and calumny."

Ignaz Semmelweis would walk in the shoes of Leopold Auenbrügger.

His book would be translated from Latin to French by the most noteworthy and influential physician of the western world: Dr. Jean-Nicolas Corvisart (1755-1821). Born in the French village of Dricourt, now in Ardennes, Corvisart was Emperor Napoleon's private physician. The physicians of Empress Maria Theresa and Napoleon Bonaparte, Gerard van Swieten and Jean-Nicolas Corvisart, would have lasting impact on the science of medicine, establishing the university as a body of state and focusing on the education of civil servants. Instead of accompanying Napoleon to Italy in 1807, Corvisart stayed behind and walked through Vienna University's spectacular botanical gardens as was

Semmelweis forty years later, and the former produced his monumental work on the human heart--*Essai sur les maladies et les lésions organiques du cœur et des gros vaisseaux.*

Semmelweis poured himself into his studies. The curricula included courses in pathological anatomy, surgery, microscopic surgery of cadaver, obstetrics (an elective, two months), on top of rounds of the medical and surgical wards. His anatomy professor, Christian Josef Berres,* intrigued him. Born in Goding, Germany, Berres was regal, charismatic. He came to his lectures in an elegant frockcoat, vest, starched high white collar, and black ascot.

He was a pioneer in photomicrography--producing photomicrographs via the daguerreotype. Berres's work had grown out of a need resulting from the cholera pandemic which, only a few years before, had taken 100,000 in Hungary, 130,000 in Egypt and 20,000 in Paris, spreading by means of steamboat traffic on rivers, including the Danube. He was conducting research on what came to be called Anthropotomy, the way the human body was built, and on the anatomy of microscopic structures. He was teaching and, at the same time, devising means to illuminate the basic substances of the human body. Right before Semmelweis's and the other students' eyes, Berres attached a camera to a microscope and took pictures and showed the results, a magnification of tissues and cells seen through the microscope. The more you see with the naked eye, unaided and aided, the more you know. Also, Semmelweis learned, you could teach and practice and research all at one and the same time.

"Doubtless he had already overstepped the wise boundaries set up by our common sense..." Dr. L.F. Destouches

And then hardly had his student completed his first year than Dr. Skoda recommended he return to Buda and continue his medical studies there. What had Semmelweis done? There is no single reported incident. He appears to have suffered from drastic mood swings, several commentators such as Drs. Destouches and Nuland have noted. Was it exhaustion? as Joseph Skoda believed, that propelled his prize student to act viciously toward fellow students who made fun of his accent and derided his being Jewish? The fact that Rokitansky and Skoda were foreigners themselves, from Czechoslovakia and Bohemia respectively, and a valued colleague Semmelweis would soon make, Dr. Ferdinand Hebra,* hailed from Moravia, all speaking German with slight accents, too, and students and visiting physicians from around the world filled the famous university's halls and rooms with all their respective languages and accents—all did not console Semmelweis. According to Dr. Destouches, he "lacked tact."

Semmelweis returned to his hometown of Buda and continued his studies in its medical school. Did his temperament swing back to a more civil plane now that he was in the setting of others of his dialect and culture, back with family, on the street seeing and hearing again that street musician with loose guitar strings, re-visiting the gardens and taking long walks in the *Füvészkert*, Budapest's main garden with thousands of plant species, Semmelweis viewing many of them with keen interest? Brother Jószef had joined their father in the spice shop and brother Fülöp had also gone into the trading business. His sister Julianna was engaged to a chemist. It's said that Semmelweis showed little patience with his teachers. Outdated lessons? And so after two years, in 1841, Semmelweis returned to Vienna and his studies there. It made perfect sense. Graduating from Vienna's medical school allowed you to practice over the entire Austrian empire, while graduating from Buda's allowed you to practice only in Budapest.

Semmelweis was allowed back to Vienna due to Skoda's diplomatic sway. He was mindful of his own tenuous position which teetered upon being a progressive medical researcher practitioner and visionary at the mercy of the Austrian empire's repressive regime as well as conservative colleagues, while, at the same time, understanding the changes that time wrought. His influence at court grew alongside his reputation as first among physicians of the empire.

Now Semmelweis needed an area of specialty. Skoda advised concentration on the possibilities of the stethoscope, for which he had shown talent. Rene Laennec*, a student of the famed Jean Corvisart, had invented the stethoscope only a few decades before, in 1816.

The story goes that Laennec, a modest young man, was embarrassed by placing his ear on a female patient's large chest in order to hear her heart sounds. She was so obese that Laennec could not listen to her heart through the intermediate layers of lipid fat. So right there in his office he took up a rolled sheet of paper and created an aural tube with which he ausculated her heart. He went on to refine his invention using wood*. Laennec writes in the preface to his classic treatise *De l'Auscultation Médiate*, published in August 1819:

"In 1816, I was consulted by a young woman laboring under general symptoms of diseased heart, and in whose case percussion and the application of the hand were of little avail on account of the great degree of fatness. The other method just mentioned [direct auscultation] being rendered inadmissible by the age and sex of the patient, I happened to recollect a simple and well-known fact in acoustics...the great distinctness with which we hear the scratch of a pin at one end of a piece of wood on applying our ear to the other. Immediately, on this suggestion, I rolled a quire of paper into a kind of cylinder and applied one end of it to the region of the heart and the other to my ear, and was not a little surprised and pleased to find that I could thereby perceive the action of the heart in a manner much more clear and distinct than I had ever been able to do by the immediate application of my ear."

Semmelweis's other great mentor Karl Rokitansky advised him to pursue extensive research on hepatic tissue.

Semmelweis responded to both advisors sharply, shocking even them. His brief respite in Buda with family and familiar surroundings had not reversed from his mood swing of "brooding intensity" to "playful, jocular, popular; a bright and jolly companion". And the fact that they were so supportive of his work did not neutralize his volatile temperament. With the result that Semmelweis stayed away from the amphitheaters and the hospital. Months passed. His thoughts had increasingly turned toward the patient as opposed to hepatic tissue and auscultations and palpitations, which, from time immemorial, had not been unable to save a single woman's life from dying of childbed fever. And throughout it all, Semmelweis experienced little peace. Brought back from sleep, from dreams in the dead of night —ding! a ring--.he opens his door a crack to a slow-moving, solemn procession, composed of a priest preceded by a sacristan who rings the viaticum rhythmically. A new mother was about to die.

Is cancer's cure to be found not solely in the laboratory but also in plain view?--A.V.

Semmelweis took long walks in the university botanical garden, passing and gazing at hundreds of species of simples, or medicinal plants, a thousand trees like the ancient Jacquin-Plane Tree, and thousands of plant species. He consulted a botanist named Bozatov, who was staunch in his belief that the future of western medicine, at least in great part, hinged on the healing properties of plants. Obsessive and resolute, Semmelweis plunged into the study of plants.

He divined herbal medicine's future as a source of healing.

In an effort to conjoin his studies of plants and their uses in medicine with his formal medical school training, Semmelweis made the outlandish thesis proposal, *On the Life of the Plants*. And it was accepted.

What great good luck if your thesis advisor is also the Director of Faculty Jury on Theses. That is exactly what happened to Semmelweis. Of all the reactionary people in the repressive government who dictated medical faculty appointments, it was Joseph Skoda who presided over Semmelweis's thesis defense. Maybe the eminent physicians and researchers such as Skoda, Rokitansky, Hebra and Kolletschka* slipped through the political cracks because they also attended members of the royal house at their bedsides, sometimes delivering their women's babies. Skoda was much needed on Semmelweis's panel, for plant and herb panaceas were largely held as so much quackery.

Joseph Skoda, after sitting like a wooden Indian, and not saying anything, uncomfortable with his position of holding all the power in mute form, he pipes up and turns to Semmelweis:

"Is there a flower whose sap can replace mercury?"

"Ah, yes. The green dye of Lilies of the Field. Willow bark. Aloe. Cilantro," answered Semmelweis.

Then Skoda asks a second question:

"Dr. Semmelweis, can you direct a few words on the delicate subject of Medicine and Sentiment?"

Semmelweis had followed the requisite guideline of writing his thesis in Latin, fourteen pages of poor Latin with which Skoda was forever patient, as he was with Semmelweis's response in a hodgepodge of German and Hungarian floral poesy, but from the heart:

"What spectacle can rejoice the heart and mind of a man more than plants. Rejoice more than these glorious flowers with their marvelous variety exhaling their delicious odors. Which furnish to our tastes the most delicious saps. Which nourish our bodies and heal it of its maladies. The spirit of plants has inspired the cohort of poets of the divine Apollo who marveled already at their countless forms. Man's reason cannot bring itself to understand such phenomena on which it can shed not light but that which natural philosophy adopts and respects. From all that lives, in fact, emanates the omnipotence of the Divine." (from *Semmelweis* by Dr. Destouches)

On that day, either in March or in May of 1844, Ignaz Philipp Semmelweis was received as a doctor of medicine in Vienna's Imperial General Hospital.

"Of all the diseases studied by dissection, the most mystifying is that of puerperal fever. From the time of Hippocrates, this disease has outnumbered in its victims more than the plague. Every aspect of post-mortem findings on diseased mothers is well-known, yet the cure remains a mystery."—Professor Karl von Rokitansky

Now that he was Dr. Semmelweis, he needed a job. He applied for an Assistantship, a position equivalent to today's Resident. Forever unpredictable, he opted first for an Assistantship not in Skoda's specialty or Rokitansky's but in Forensic Pathology, admiring a physician of his generation who was also a student of Rokitansky's, Jacob Kolletschka, professor of Forensic Pathology. Semmelweis had to know that any legal finding that could implicate the Austrian empire would be summarily quashed. Nevertheless, though Kolletschka also admired Semmelweis, there was no job for him in his department, and his application was for an Assistantship was denied. Later on, Jacob Kolletschka would play a major though tragic role in Semmelweis's discoveries. *Then* he turned to Joseph Skoda. What could have been more wonderful than making the rounds alongside the great diagnostician? What could have been more useful than correlating clinical findings with the pathological changes that caused them? Skoda was described as "remarkable, shrewd, sagacious," and the Chief Internist had recently published his *Treatise on Auscultation*, which, according to many, consisted of as much quackery as belief in the medicinal uses of the poppy seed. Skoda had to be practical and prudent and stay in line within certain rules. A competition for his Assistantship was opened. Semmelweis entered but Skoda had promised the position to a physician more senior to Semmelweis, Dr. Gustav Loebl, and gave it to him.

Patience, Skoda advised Semmelweis. The next competition would soon be opened.

But patience requires time and his father was ill, and income from the spice business was suffering. Hurry and open a practice of your own, his family advised.

Semmelweis turned to his primary mentor and instructor, Karl von Rokitansky. The great pathologist directed him to the field he knew best, surgery. Nine out of ten surgeries ended in infection or death, and so little wonder that Surgery warranted only three or four official posts. But while he waited for a post to open, Semmelweis was invited to join Rokitansky in the surgical theater. He spent days, months--two years—there. It was a most productive period of waiting. While the causes of childbed fever remained a mystery, while new mothers died in an agonizing manner around the world on a daily basis, transforming almost instantaneously from joyous new mothers to unimaginable such mothers about to lose their lives and, along with them, their babies, the body of such a tragic new mother who had recently died was up in Autopsy. As he had at that fateful time when he audited a demonstration by Joseph Skoda, a fever victim, and the next morning was drawn to follow up and walked up to Autopsy, Semmelweis stood side by side with Karl von Rokitansky, his stiff white shirt sleeves rolled up, black frockcoat hanging on a hook by the door. His skilled bare hand makes a neat incision in the abdomen....

The famous pathological anatomist often quoted his forerunner, the Bolognese physician Giovanni Morgagni:

"If you want to understand disease, you must identify its seat, the place in which it begins." Only from dedicating his life to medical research could Morgagni have spoken of organs in highly human terms. "Listen, my friends, listen to the cries of the suffering organs." *

Semmelweis listened. He listened to women. He listened to the cries of new mothers and their newborns. He observed. He calculated. He wondered. Young mother after young mother, more than any other category of hospital deaths, wheeled into Autopsy. Semmelweis awaits on the third floor, horrified. My god, so young! Only days ago filled with such joy. Babies, too. Babies who died along with their mothers, they are wheeled in, too. Not as many, but newborns all the same. Autopsy performed on a newborn....One by tragic one, from January to June 1845, of approximately 1700 births, 93 mothers died from childbed fever. 93 who would never see their babies more than a few days old. Accompanied by the agony of knowing in a flash moment that their babies, if they survived, would have only tragic memories of their mothers.

One of the most famous cases of childbed fever up until his time was that of the famous author and women's rights advocate, Mary Wollstonecraft. She died giving birth to a girl, whom she'd named Mary, and Mary grew to remember her circumstance of birth, saying, "I killed my mother," and then she went on to marry a famous poet, Percy Bysshe Shelley and, when still a teenager, wrote a book about a monster called Frankenstein.

While associated with Rokitansky, Semmelweis associated with physicians from all parts of Europe, Asia and America. They were attracted by the high rate of death due to puerperal fever. They came to the *Allgemeine Krankenhaus* to witness, report and, later on, practice what Rokitansky showed them.

Semmelweis becomes as skilled an observer as dissector. The identification of symptoms with their organs of origin was not enough. Patterns of findings were as important as the findings themselves. Tirelessly, enthusiastically, he dissected the cadavers of new mothers recently deceased from puerperal fever.

Throughout his work of dissecting corpses, he listened to his colleagues provide all sorts of reasons for Fever deaths. He told his friend Lajos Markusovszky:

"Everything they are trying to do here seems to me quite futile, deaths follow one another with regularity. They go on operating, however, without really seeking to discover why one patient succumbs rather than another in identical circumstances."

Semmelweis gave a brilliant exam and, on 26 November 1846, was appointed Master of Surgery.

But there were no vacancies. Once again, Semmeweis was without a post.

Then the progressive Skoda and Rokitansky guided their protégée to the relatively new specialty, Obstetrics and the lying-in pavilions. Midwifery had moved from the home to the Second lying-in clinic, while medical students staffed the First. Johann Klein was Director of Obstetrics and he needed an assistant. Skoda and Rokitansky offered him Semmelweis, and Klein, unfamiliar with the character of the young physician, accepted.

Obstetrics--that or nothing.

One of the greatest scientists of all time came to his métier purely by a divine act of attrition.

It is Tuesday 27 February 1844, Dr. Ignaz Semmelweis's first day as Assistant of Obstetrics.

At the crack of dawn perform autopsies on his patients who died during the night. Death so close upon dreams, upon awakening. His sun rises on the wings of a new mother's death, a newborn's cries. Take in the sights and smells in Autopsy.

Examine patients in preparation for Director Johann Klein's rounds. Prepare summary reports in his best German. Supervise difficult deliveries. The labor and joy of life commingle with death. He could never have dreamed that a new mother come down with childbed fever would be a patient of his. In his First lying-in Clinic, Semmelweis finds twenty to thirty women lying quietly joyous from having just given birth. At least six will die of childbed fever in short order. His duties include teaching a course in obstetrics. For the first time, look out into the faces of students and feel their eyes watching, ears listening, hearts soaring…hear himself. According to his colleague and best friend, Lajos Markusovszky, who audited his lectures, Semmelweis "was gruff…did not suffer fools lightly…passionate at the rostrum…expounded his teaching with conviction…not only fights for the truth but vouches for it with his life." He held practical operative exercises on cadavers before the afternoon rounds at four p.m. because, in the morning, students were otherwise engaged. For such exercises to follow the afternoon rounds, it was already too dark. Much of Semmelweis's practical work occurred during the daylight hours, his nocturnal hours reserved for personal torment. Lastly but perhaps most important in regard to his discoveries, Semmelweis served as Clerk of Records.

Clerk of Records. Admit and register each and every pregnant woman who has come to Vienna Imperial Hospital to give birth. Look into each and every face. Hear each and every voice. Record each and every name and background, father if known. These pregnant women whom Semmelweis was the first to see remain anonymous, known solely to this Clerk of Records. Anonymous women dominate the cast of characters in the saga of Semmelweis's life. A host of anonymous women who die and survive and their anonymous babies who also die and survive.

Survive or not, they are no more developed than the data Semmelweis recorded of them. They are the images Semmelweis carried along on his journey. Careful records were kept at Vienna Hospital, that came with being the largest in the world, staffed with the most notable professors and physicians. These records end in a basement in a morass of cobwebs, what they represent in the flesh lost to history. There is no record of any surviving mother or child come back to visit with him, thank him. Semmelweis and only Semmelweis carried their private histories and images for the rest of his life. They were mostly single teenagers from the "comfortless classes," Semmelweis described them, in need and suffering, deprived of emotional support and had led generally "unhappy and dissolute lives." They earned their bread throughout pregnancy by hard work. Cut off from family, alone, often living on the street. Vienna, then, was the center of Austria's railway network, and the capital city had become the hub of migrant railway workers and their offspring. Term would come upon many of these women suddenly. There was no time to entertain any option other than to be taken to the Imperial Hospital…placed in one or the other of its maternity clinics. At the same time, these young pregnant women knew what was what. The number of deaths attributed to the Fever traveled through the streets like wild fire. They could smell death. The stench of decaying putrid organic matter emanating from the lying-in wards' sick room and the morgue was a major factor in the early history of the field of obstetrics.

After the day's last rounds, Semmelweis spends hours in the university library researching trends, statistics, puerperal fever's history. In his room, by the light of a flickering gas lamp, picture Dr. Semmelweis into the wee hours reading, analyzing, note taking by flickering gaslight. Restless in his chair, hand running through his thinning hair, he poures over numbers. They show little consistency. 23 mothers dead in January. 13 in February. 20 in May. There had to be a consistent, all-embracing pathology. For the Miracle of Life there had to be a cure.

He pours over conclusions posited by individual obstetricians and countless official commission reports. During the puerperal epidemic of 1774, which decimated the Hotel-Dieu in Paris, Louis XVI convoked a commission that decided that the mother's milk was the disease's cause. All maternity wards were closed, and wet nurses were isolated. He studies the observations of obstetricians as far away as Philadelphia and Jerusalem, Hugh Lennox Lodge* and Scholtz respectively. Most known childbed fever epidemics were limited to Central Europe. Generally, cold and moist lands appeared especially afflicted. England was more afflicted than France. The same holds for cities located on the banks of large rivers—Vienna, for example. On the other hand, reported Brydon, women in Sicily seldom became ill after delivery. In his letters, Savary reported from Egypt that nursing diseases were entirely unknown there. Semmelweis studies data from maternity clinics in the United States. They were independent, removed from general hospitals, and students occupied themselves solely with obstetrics. Some causal theories he could eliminate outright.

A Vengeful Goddess caused puerperal fever.

Most new mothers were loose women deserved of the harshest of punishments while preserving the purity of the race. In addition to peeling walls, contaminated air and dirty bed sheets caused the Fever.

Fever deaths were ascribed to "thickened pus," "benign pus," "laudable pus."

Puerperal fever was caused by impurities arising in the colon, perhaps worsened by the overuse of purgatives.

The priest's bell trumpeting his arrival to administer last rites at yet another mother's deathbed filled the other expectant mothers in the lying-in wards with terrible anxiety.

Too much blood in the circulation.

Disturbances caused by the pregnant uterus.

Protracted labor.

Decreased weight caused by the emptying of the uterus.

Wounding of the uterus' inner surface in delivery.

Volume of secreted milk.

Seduced women were always an easy sacrifice.

Delivery in the presence of men embarrassed the women and their offended modesty triggered puerperal fever.

Victims of the scourge, Semmelweis noted, were depicted as dissipated and yet "are assumed to possess such tender modesty as never appears in the higher classes."

Over and over, Semmelweis witnessed firsthand the primordial fear that prospective mothers felt throughout pregnancy. Even women who'd had children before were afraid. This time, with this child, they would pay with their life. Particularly upon reaching term, fear of death embittered the woman's life. Of the two lying-in clinics, the First and Second, it was held that the First's mortality rate was higher due to the obstetricians' examining patients in a rougher manner than the student midwives of the Second. Semmelweis dismissed this cause, saying:

"If inserting the finger, however roughly, into the vagina and to the adjacent parts of the uterus— already widened and extended by pregnancy—was sufficient to cause damages leading to so horrific a condition, then surely the passage of the baby's body through the birth canal must cause damage so much worse that every birth would end in the mother's death."

The prevailing opinion was that winter was the season most conducive to outbreaks of childbed fever. More women gave birth during the winter months, perhaps because more couples made love at their outset and throughout the spring season. But according to Semmelweis, who would spend a great deal of time on the issue of epidemic espousal as the Fever's main cause, this was the safest posture. Since no one could discover the disease's cause, doctors were powerless and therefore blameless.

Women at their most vulnerable at the hands, and mercy, of men.

About these men, Semmelweis said: "Perhaps such persons fear that upon recognizing the truth, a great guilt is imputed."

As it turned out, it was precisely the "great guilt" that Dr. Semmelweis imputed upon such persons that eventually moved them to get rid of him.

The Lying-in Clinics

it is four p.m. and the doors to the Second Clinic have just closed and those of the First opened.

Pregnant women make a mad dash to the hospital for admission to the First. Some opt to deliver right there on the street, or in some back alleyway, rather than risk assignment to that First Clinic. Its high mortality rate was their key source, their guidance. Thus far that year, and it was still young, of 2,000 births, more than 250 new mothers had died. In the First Clinic, of approximately 500 deliveries, 45 had already died. In the Second clinic, the rate is about one-third less, 15 deaths per 300 births. The mortality rate was much greater in the First Clinic than in the Second. Actually, the mortality rate in the First Clinic was even higher, due to the fact that some women who got very sick were moved out of Maternity and into the hospital population proper and, if they died, their deaths were not counted along with deaths in the maternity wards. Family, if any, and passersby had to virtually drag some of these worried pregnant women to the hospital. Some women in labor opted to deliver not only on the street but also on the glacis, a medieval fortification of a broad network that slopes away from the city.

Sweating, breathless, women holding their bellies file into Admissions. They stand in line. The Clerk of Records, Dr. Ignaz Semmelweis, sits behind a desk.

"Clinic #1. Next, please..."

Some kneel and wring their hands and implore him:

"Please, assign me to the Second Clinic, not the First!"

"One woman," Semmelweis wrote, "was stricken suddenly with labor pains in the street about five o'clock in the afternoon…she had no home…she hastened to the hospital but realized right away that she was too late…here was this woman pleading, begging to be admitted to Bartsch's clinic [the Second] on her life and on behalf of her other children. She was refused this favor. She was not the only one."

It's his singular privilege to look these panicky women in the eye, only to see many of them a few days later, deceased, up in Autopsy.

The majority of women went ahead to the First Clinic, risking their lives. Where could they possibly go now? In return for agreeing to have their bodies used for teaching purposes, birthing was free. If something happened to them, their orphaned babies had spots in the foundling home across the road.

Women of wealth did not have their bodies used for teaching purposes.

Semmelweis experienced—"…maternity patients with abnormally high pulse rates, bloated stomachs and dry tongues (in other words, very ill with puerperal fever), still insisting hours before death that they were perfectly healthy, because they knew that treatment by a medical student or attending physician in the First Clinic was the forerunner of death."

The facts as these mainly teenage fearful pregnant women knew them constituted the premise upon which Semmelweis proceeded with his work.

His superior Johann Klein's unwavering position in regard to the causes of puerperal fever was the popular causal theory of the day: "atmospheric-cosmic-terrestrial influences". To wit:

damaging particles in the air blanketed the countryside and then entered the predisposed woman through the retention and absorption of moisture.

It was Semmelweis's misfortune that Johann Klein was in the powerful, influential position of Director, appointed on the heels of the Congress of Vienna more than twenty years before by government ministers who assured that their appointees kept to the official line. As a result, Klein restored the standard curriculum. Students learned to do obstetric exams by using cadavers. Constraints were relaxed on students' and doctors' internal exams during labor and forceps deliveries. The mortality rate of new mothers immediately soared to 7.45 percent.

After two months of further study, and taking the course in Obstetrics a second time, he passed all necessary tests and, on 10 January 1846, Ignaz

Philipp Semmelweis was accepted as a Doctor of Obstetrics.

Differences

"Only the great number of the dead was an undoubted reality."—Dr. Ignaz Semmelweis

Semmelweis proceeds with his work by asking, How is it that for many years these "atmospheric-cosmic-terrestrial conditions" affected patients in the First Clinic and spared those in the Second? The same conditions must operate with minimal variation in the Second Clinic as well. Both clinics have one common ante-room, and their construction was the same. The two pavilions were adjacent to one another and shared a few facilities. Atmospheric differences were the same in both. The First Clinic's high mortality rate, one recent commission reported, was because its patients are unmarried women of the most hopeless class, women accustomed to earn their bread in want and misery, amid conditions which produced great and constant depression of spirit.

Semmelweis counters: if this were true, the mortality rate in the Second Division would be exactly the same, for the same class of patients is admitted to it. This was fact, for he was the one who admitted. He was the one who knew.

The higher mortality of the First Clinic was also ascribed to the wounded modesty of the poor, young, afflicted women going through the process of giving birth in the presence of men.

In his role as Clerk of Records, Semmelweis interviewed many of these women and got to know their thinking, their feelings.

"Not many were troubled with a sense of shame," he said.

In the First Clinic, it was put forward, patients got up too soon after labor. They would do so a few hours after labor's completion, then walk to the beds allotted to them in the lying-in ward, a considerable distance away. Weak patients and operation cases were carried, but the patient after normal labor had to walk.

The arrangements in the Second Clinic were exactly the same. The disadvantages of uninterrupted clinical instruction, the communication of the rooms reserved for infected cases with the ordinary lying-in wards, the free intercourse of the nursing staff attending the fever cases with those in attendance on the normal puerperae, alleged to be factors in producing the mortality rate--all were matters common to both clinics.

Allso, in his clinic, the First, one woman would fall victim while several women in the neighboring beds, to right and left, remained well. Occasionally, patients in whole rows of beds sickened about the same time. In the Second Clinic, patients who became ill were always scattered, never in rows.

The occurrence of cases in rows, called *reihenweise,* arose out of the spread of the contagion* from bed to bed.

Then a Commission reported that puerperal illness was the result of injuries to the genital organs produced by examinations of the medical students in the First Clinic for purposes of instruction. Semmelweis pointed out that, in the course of their training, such examinations were also made by pupil midwives in the Second Clinic.

Director Klein had the answer. The foreign students. It was the foreign students who caused the higher rate of death in his First Clinic. A meeting was called. Skoda and Rokitansky in attendance. Semmelweis was there, too.

Klein at the rostrum declares that the higher rate of death in his clinic, the First, is due to the foreign students making examinations of pregnant women in a rougher manner than the midwives of the Second. These students were "foreign" in the sense of being educated outside of Austria, who then continued at the University of Vienna. Students who completed their education at the *"Hochschule,"* or an Austrian university, were considered "native."

Semmelweis stands up.

"Why not rid ourselves of all students."

Easily imagine Drs. Skoda and Rokitansky slowly shaking their heads.

A surge of hatred began to surround Semmelweis's name, especially in the person of his superior, Johann Klein.

Director Klein went ahead and set in motion foreign student expulsions. Why not? He—any attending physician--could never be blamed as long as there was no cure. Acting on his improvable supposition would garner results equally improvable. And so, twenty out of forty-two medical students, chosen with straws, were extradited to their respective countries.

The mortality rate from childbed fever did diminish in December (1846). But during the first three months of 1847, it rose in April to over 18 percent and in May to over 12 percent.

Foreign students as a group were not causing the difference in mortality rates. Weighing upon Semmelweis also was the disrespect shown by hospital employees to personnel in his clinic.

And then night after night there was the tolling of the priest's bell, first afar then closer…closer until the haunting figure of the slow-moving priest about to render Last Rites to another dying woman was right outside his door.

In the morning, along with the rising sun, Semmelweis climbs the endless steps to Autopsy.

Suddenly, a light however dim.

His predecessor, Dr. Eduard Lumpe, had ventured that most cases of childbed fever were caused by harmful miasms generated within the First Clinic itself. It admitted more patients than the Second and so the First was overcrowded. Therefore, the harmful miasms were not dispelled as readily as in the Second.

"If overcrowding were the cause of death," Semmelweis responded, "mortality in the Second Section would have been larger because the Second was more crowded than the First."

Nevertheless, Dr. Lumpe was on to something. The answer was right there before their eyes. The cause of childbed fever and its means of prevention which had eluded scientists and killed new mothers famous and not-so-famous, now and since time immemorial--that cause and prevention resided nowhere else in the world, in no other place, in no other maternity clinic than in Vienna's Imperial Hospital. Further, it was within the confines of Vienna's imperial hospital's lying-in First Clinic.

The Truth was in the palms of Ignaz Semmelweis's hands.

In examining the extant causes of puerperal fever, Semmelweis displayed his humanity, fierce determination, tender heart, natural intelligence, sense of logic and sarcastic bent. At the same time, his restless energy and constant criticism of orthodox opinions, especially those of his immediate superior, were the subject of conversation and criticism of this Jewish Assistant from a small town in Budapest.

Uniformity

"One must try every day to bring to the surface from the depths of one's being, a sound, an accent, a fossil or vegetable residue of something that is not pure thought, that is or is not feeling, but something curious, a regret, something sincere, anatomized and no more."— Italo Svevo, Diary

From the depths of his empathetic being Semmelweis brought to the surface the idea of equalizing the conditions of the two clinics that his brilliant mind could muster: physical, environmental, vegetal. Then he would have to wait. If results showed that the death rates in both wards were the same, he could isolate one condition and then another.

He makes sure that the same food is served to patients of both sections. Popular dishes at that time in Vienna were a clear beef soup, *Rindsuppe,* and *Tafelspitz,* beef boiled in broth. He works to see that the same laundry contractor served both sections and that the two sections are equally ventilated. He discontinues supine deliveries in the First Clinic in favor of deliveries in a lateral position which was customary in the Second. He wrote,

"I did not believe that the supine position was so detrimental that additional deaths could be attributed to its use. But in the second section, deliveries were performed from a lateral position and the patients were healthier."

He canvasses hospital personnel for the reasons they acted in a hostile manner to the First Clinic's staff, heaping blame on staff for the higher rate of deaths. He considers low morale, loss of focus on duty to perhaps a higher death rate. Why would personnel behave in this way? Their family members die in that clinic as well? Whatever the unearthly reason, the prejudice haunts Semmelweis at least for the next ten years, at which time he wrote:

"The disrespect that employees showed toward personnel of the First Clinic made me so miserable that life seemed worthless. Everything was in question. Everything seemed inexplicable. Everything was doubtful."

Ding--that unceasing bell. Women in term, waiting--would the priest come for her next?

"The priest's bell has a terrifying effect on my nerves. I groan within for the victim soon to fall to an unknown cause," Semmelweis confessed to his friend Lajos Markuszovsky.

The impression is that for the two years Semmelweis resided in Vienna, he did not leave the hospital grounds. Not a pleasant walk outside the flowering grounds nor a visit to a colleague or acquaintance. There's no hint of an amorous life. Not a beer with one of the lay nurses. He dwelled within the space of the disease he would conquer. The life of Semmelweis emerges in a purely claustrophobic manner, tied irrevocably to one new mother after another, hundreds upon hundreds of them, many of whom lived to see how their children turned out, many not. When he slept, the odor of decomposing animal matter played around his nostrils. As noted, the nocturnal tinkling of the priest's ominous bell tormented him.

The imperial hospital's chapel was located such that when the priest was summoned to administer last rites for a deceased woman in the Second Clinic, he could go directly to the Sick Room. But when summoned to the First Clinic, Father had to pass through five other rooms, the Sick Room being sixth in line from the chapel.

Imagine Semmelweis goes to the rectory. The door opens to a priest in a black vestment whom he does not recognize. Squinting, this priest peers deep into Semmelweis's soul.

"Yes?"

Fact is, Semmelweis appealed to "the compassion of the servant of God," he would write, that he come to the First Clinic's Sick Room without bells and without passing through the other five rooms. Thus, no one other than those poor new mothers in the Sick Room would know of his presence…about another imminent death. In order to eliminate the fear in the hearts of healthy pregnant women, this servant of God went on to do as the doctor requested.

Then Semmelweis waits…waits some more. For the work he undertook he had to develop, as the cliché says, the patience of a saint. Had his efforts brought Clinic #1 and Clinic #2 in line as to the death rate? What consolation, what winning feeling could there have been even if he had?

The priest's compassionate detour made no difference in the death rate. Nor, it turned out, does Semmelweis find a single satisfactory cause for the differences between the First and Second Clinics.

"I was bewildered. I was tormented."
—Semmelweis

He wrote to Lajos:

"My dear Markusovszky, my good friend, my kind supporter--I must confess to you that my life is a living hell, that always the thought of death for my patients is unbearable to me, especially as it arrives between the two great joys of living, that of being young and that of giving life."

Like the Assistants before him, Semmelweis's tenure as Assistant was for two years. In less time--November 1846--he was compelled to withdraw in favor of his predecessor, Dr. Franz Breit, who reclaimed his former post. Most likely, Dr. Klein compelled Breit to do so. Rules applied except in the case of Dr. Ignaz Semmelweis. Performance of his official duties did not amount to keeping him on. His indefatigable work, commitment and personal torment in regard to woman after woman dying of childbed fever amounted to an official nothing.

Once again, Semmelweis was on the move. One of the first of many obstacles was placed in his way of continuing his work in behalf of pregnant women, new mothers and newborns. He decided not to return home nor stay in Vienna. He would pursue his studies and work in another country, another culture. Ireland, he would go to Dublin's large maternity hospital as a way of retracing the steps and successful methods of his clinic's first director, Dr. Johann Boër,* Dr. Klein's predecessor. The cure was not only right before his eyes but also couched in history.

Maria Theresa's heir, Josef II, had decreed that in order for Vienna Hospital's obstetrics department to be the finest in Europe, "it must have a cosmopolitan director," and so he appointed Dr. Johann Boër and sent him straightaway to study in England and France. After a year, Boër returned to Vienna and was named professor of midwifery and director of the lying-in-hospital, adopting gentle techniques and natural methods of the British accoucheurs. How could he extend Dr. Boër's knowledge and work? Semmelweis spent the winter of 1846-'47 learning the English language. At least he would sound foreign in a foreign country.

Then, the unforeseen reared an ugly face. He received two letters, one close upon the heels of the other, the first announced that his father had passed away, whereupon he returned to Buda, and the second, that his mother had died.

"Let us not underestimate the influence of his mother's death on his life."-- Dr. Sherwin B. Nuland

From Vienna to his hometown Buda in Hungary covered 250 kilometers, south and east back to Pressburg, then across the Danube again. Semmelweis sits in his rambling coach, pensive, looking out to terrain covered before but which now takes on a somber hue.

Home.... He's at home walking along Tában's cobblestone streets, filled as always with the gypsies' plaintive songs and fast melodies, and the hand-clapping and clicking of wooden spoons. That poor musician with his guitar of four loose strings--is he still there? The organ plays from St. Stephen's, in whose shadow continues to loom his house.

Elder brother József had joined their father in the store. Brother Fülüp also became a trader in spices. Sister Julianna was still engaged.

Who can say the nature of his mother's influence? Solely that shortly after his mother, Terézia Müller, passed away, Semmelweis made his great discoveries.

Part III: BREAKTHROUGH

"Destiny chose me to be a missionary of truth as to the means that must be taken to avoid and to combat the puerperal scourge."—Dr. Ignaz Semmelweis

Semmelweis saw all that is worth in women.—A.V.

He did not go to Dublin and investigate and learn from its great maternity hospital, because after serving the last four months of 1846, his replacement, Dr. Breit, was named professor of obstetrics at the University of Tübingen. Semmelweis picked up at the imperial hospital where he had left off those four months earlier. Certainly, Klein did not welcome him back, but his teachers and mentors Drs. Skoda and Rokitansky had gained influence with the education minister and at court. After all, in addition to first-rate obstetricians to insure their divine rights, the royal family and courtesans needed top-notch internists and surgeons. The great physicians and teachers campaigned for Semmelweis's return as Assistant of Obstetrics, and that is what happened.

The Exchange

Life is about people so Semmelweis shifted emphasis from the two lying-in clinics' similarities and differences to the human aspect. To the personnel of the two clinics: students and attending physicians who examined and delivered in the First clinic, midwives in the Second.

"Deaths in the First Clinic were not caused by epidemic influences but by endemic and yet unknown factors," Semmelweis wrote about this exact time.

A statistic from 1842 to the present spring day in 1847 that captured his attention was that maternity hospitals that were not teaching hospitals, as was his, or that trained only midwives, which his was not, had a lower mortality rate. This fact was as true in Strasbourg as it was in Vienna. Also, a colleague shared an observation to which Semmelweis listened: "The fewer deaths in Bartsch's (the Second) pavilion is due to the clumsiness of the medical students examining and delivering in the

First. This must be the real cause of the fatal inflammation."

Medical students and visiting physicians examined the women in the First Clinic, from the time they arrived, throughout labor and delivery.

An experiment strikes him. Exchange the midwives of the Second Clinic with the students of the First. He received permission to make the switch, most likely through Joseph Skoda's influence. Now midwives examined and delivered in the First Clinic while medical students did same in the Second. Again Semmelweis waits...two weeks...a month... Finally, results: from June through December (1847), of the 1,841 deliveries in the First Clinic, 56 new mothers died. The mortality rate of 3% is comparable to the death rate of the Second Clinic.

Death followed the students.

He considers a few variables. The practices of midwives have no contact with cadavers. They do not bloody their hands. They do not go from Dissection to Delivery. They practice on the Phantom instead of on a cadaver. Another variable concerns the women who deliver on the street. They and their babies manage to escape death by the Fever.

"To me," he wrote, "it appeared logical that patients who experienced street births would become ill at least as frequently as those who delivered in the clinic....What protected those who delivered outside the clinic from these destructive unknown endemic influences?"

He'd found the answer. Medical students did not attend to the pregnant women on the street.

"The fact is," he wrote to Lajos, "I am searching in our own clinic and we need to look nowhere else."

He scrutinizes these medical students, foreign and native, their comings and goings, their habits. Waits outside Autopsy, watches silently, anonymously. He must be a clandestine observer. He must have them not make the slightest change in their routines. Perform autopsies on recently deceased new mothers, bloodied hands reaching into the genitals reeking and oozing with pus and ochor, then wash their hands with soap and water cursorily, which some skip, then they descend as if to hell to his clinic, the First. From a dark corner, he watches students examine pregnant women with hands washed hastily. Then he goes to Clinic #2 and observes hands of midwives untarnished with the byproducts of Autopsy.

After an autopsy of his own, and after he washes his own hands with soap and water, he brings his hands to his nose. Inhale, again, breathe in. There it is, that ever-present odor of cadaveric particles which had greeted him on his first day at Vienna Hospital and lingered throughout school, those two years operating beside Rokitansky, and played around his nostrils while he slept. It shot out to the priest who passed with his tinkling bell and then rushed back in to his bed. The odor of the process of mortal death was the natural odor of his wing of the hospital, certainly the Dead Room, Autopsy, Dissection. After an hour, Dr. Semmelweis inhales again. Still there....A second hour--the malodor lingers, sometimes for a longer time, sometimes shorter. If this is so, it also has not left the hands of medical students and attending physicians of the First Clinic, as well as those of attendants of all the maternity clinics around the world who first work on cadavers. He tells Lajos:

"Cadaveric particles can be detected by their odor. They transfer from the corpse to the hands and remain despite soap and water washings. Then these same hands examine a woman approaching term and then deliver. In the end, dear friend, it is not the students who cause the Fever. It can be anyone, including myself--you, her, him and him-- whoever carries cadaveric particles on the hands."

"Deodorize the hands," he says at this time. "The whole problem is there."

Semmelweis smelled germs fifty years before Pasteur saw them.

Hardly into the second year of his Assistantship, Dr. Ignaz Philipp Semmelweis laid the foundation on which to discover the causes of puerperal fever--and infection in general.

Chlorine,* he knew, was used for decades as an efficient means of ridding objects of their noxious smells. And so, after hours, colleagues, students and midwives having gone home, the hospital silent, a few lay nurses attending, and accompanied by history and his long shadow, he goes into the university laboratory and concocts a chloride solution. Takes some up to his next autopsy and, afterwards, washes his hands with it. Waits...inhales...breathe deeply. Yes--the odor is gone. Then he goes around Vienna in search of washstands, bowls and pitchers. He searches in the famous Danhauser Furniture Factory....He's a scientist in a china shop. He comes upon washstands made of cherry wood, ceramic bowls and pitchers. But they are expensive. Local carpenters, he's told, copy Danhauser's wares. Danhauser was also a well-known painter, especially his fantasy regarding another Hungarian, Franz Liszt.

Then Semmelweis goes in search of these cheaper bowls and pitchers. He finds a few, buys them. With his own money? Hails a coach and two, loads and makes several trips to and from the hospital. What is not imagined is that somehow he gains permission or, perhaps, goes ahead without it, to set up washstands and bowls into which he pours what he calls *chlorina liquida*, a diluted concentration of chlorine, and places them on stands strategically, outside the entrances and exits of Dissection and Autopsy and the First and Second Lying-in Clinics. Now colleagues, students and midwives could rid their hands of noxious odors before and after examining and delivering. He is an opposite Dr. Frankenstein, mad with life, yes, but life of a very different kind, not of a false, prevaricated, return to, but life to go on as intended for a living beautiful vulnerable woman, pregnant with life and her healthy child.   He tells each and every attending physician and student, "Wash your hands thoroughly with the provided solution of chlorine."

At some point after a dissection, he looks at his hands. Spicules of infected matter has gotten under his fingernails. Into the lab once again and he creates one of the first, if not *the,* prototype of the surgical nail brush.

Hand-washing design ©Dave Barry

Again he waits…. The next month, the mortality rate plummeted 15%. Encouraged, he sets up more washstands, which required more and more chlorine. Chlorine was expensive, so back in the laboratory he substitutes a solution of chloride of lime. Finally: from June through December (1847), of the 1,841 deliveries in the First Clinic, 56 new mothers died. The mortality rate of 3% is comparable to that of the Second Clinic.

"Intellectually, this Klein was a poor individual, self-centered and strictly mediocre. Barely had he had the time to consider the truth about puerperal fever than he became determined to stifle this truth by all means, by every influence at his disposal."—Dr. L.F Destouches

Not only stifle this truth by all means available but Klein was out to acquire credit for the cause and cure and, at the same time, work to get rid of his brilliant, rambunctious Assistant.

Semmelweis watches, trembling at the hospital's front door. Klein arrives. "Sir I have installed washstands, bowls and pitchers at the entrance to the lying-in clinics, including ours. Physicians as well as students have been asked to wash their hands. At this stage, it is a precaution. Will, you also, sir, wash your hands with the solution provided?"

Klein was seized with the determination to suppress Semmelweis's discoveries that day and every day until the end of Semmelweis's life.

"What is the basis of this hand washing?" asks Director Klein, continuing to walk, Semmelweis keeping up.

"Current results show a decrease in rate of death in our clinic, sir. It is equal to that of Bartsch's. Further evidence will follow in the ensuing months. In the meantime, I have no such scientific basis."

"Well, then…." and he shakes his head.

Semmelweis, lacking tact and worse, nerves frayed from sleepless nights, shivering, sweating, teeth and fists clenched, right there at the front door, his Director a few feet in front of him, Semmelweis flies into a verbal and physical rage—

"Fool!" "Idiot!"

Providing Director Klein with the reason to get rid of him.

Professors Skoda and Rokitansky were aware that, just as Klein would not allow his Assistant Semmelweis to succeed, he was not about to keep his opposition to him restricted to himself. Klein would spread Semmelweis's negative profile of an impetuous, arrogant Assistant. Klein appealed to the Minister of Education, who certainly got an earful. The very next day after the confrontation, on 20 October 1846, Dr. Semmelweis was dismissed summarily.

Nevertheless, Chief Internist Joseph Skoda adopted a diplomatic stance that could, in the end, restore Semmelweis's position. He believed in Semmelweis and also knew that Klein wielded great favor in Court. Once Physician to the Imperial Family, which did not forget him, Skoda decided to use his influence but not at this precise moment. Let the world turn a few times, the dust to settle, Klein to calm down and be appeased and appear in the right. And then he would use his contacts to restore

Semmelweis to his former post. Skoda contacts Lajos Markusovszky, who knew about all that had transpired.

"Take your friend Semmelweis out of town for a while…"

"A trip to Venice," Lajos suggests, to which idea Semmelweis was not averse.   Later on, he wrote: "I hoped the Venetian art treasures would revive my mind and spirits, which had been so seriously affected by my experiences in the maternity hospital."

At a commission hearing before Semmelweis was scheduled to leave, Klein put forth that it was the age of their building that contributed to the high mortality rate in his section, not this rigmarole of his Assistant about hand washings.

Someone stood up. It was Semmelweis. "Your building was older when Dr. Boër was director and his mortality rate was practically nil."

Get out of town, indeed, so in early spring of 1847, Ignaz and his good friend Lajos rented a coach and set out for Venice, Italy. The trip took six days by coach over the Alps. You could see the horses' steamy breaths, they were working hard. Time for the good friends to assess. Ways of coexisting with Director Klein. Chances of working with Professor Bartsch in the Second Clinic. Going back home to Buda and starting up a medical practice. Semmelweis was in his mid-thirties now. Accounts of his life thus far do not include a single instance of romance, either back in Buda or in Vienna. And it had been Lajos's idea to go to Venice, the land of romance, of Casanova de Seingalt and the Bridge of Sighs and immortal painters such as Titian and Tintoretto. The good Catholic, child-producing, racist empress Maria Theresa had outlawed prostitution, shipping women of the night and other "antisocial" people, possibly gay men and women and those with criminal records and, if her path could possibly have crossed with that of the Jew Semmelweis, him, too, to Romania. Which edict failed to eliminate the oldest profession, so just about then, in1850, Dr. Semmelweis was happy to hear that Dr. Nusser of the Vienna police suggested that prostitutes be required to register with the police, receive medical examinations twice a week, and obtain special health certificates.

Women of easy virtue, at various stages of his life, no two ever the same, join the pregnant women Semmelweis checked in and examined and delivered, in the realm of anonymity.

The trip from Vienna to Venice *ordinarily* took six days, but, as it often was in the life of Ignaz Semmelweis, very little was ordinary. The road over the Alps was blocked by snow, so they detoured to Trieste. Trieste is called the Riviera on the Adriatic, for it rests along that sea and you ascend the Karst Plateau 1500 feet above sea level and glance below and out to the great sparkling Adriatic. Lajos and

Ignaz stayed a day in Treviso. Dante Alighieri described Treviso as "the place where the Sile and the Cagnan go hand in hand." The two rivers joined and circled the town, their waters running side by side. Stand on the serene bank of the Riviera Garibaldi and see the two streams not yet commingled: the Sile sleek and calm, alongside the Cagnan's turbulent flow. The great sage's description of these rivers can apply to Semmeweis's turbulent nature: calm and focused alongside irascible and unpredictable. On to Venice.

Venice

In Venice, Semmelweis exhibited another quite different side of his diverse nature, not the "brooding, caustic, self-wounding" Semmelweis of Vienna but the bon-vivant, the romantic, the Semmelweis full of spontaneous joie-de-vivre. Of course, aspects of his character co-existed everywhere and in himself all the time. History's creation of a character. Venice is a fleeting breath of fresh air for him, far from being in the constant way of disease and death.

Descriptions of his character present an active man, spontaneous, passionate, given to extremes.

"Extraordinarily good and totally generous," Dr. L.F. Destouches describes him.

"Bel nuit, ô nuit d'amour...'—Goethe

According to Goethe, who had lived life fully in Italy, had a son born and die there and buried his ashes in Rome's Protestant Cemetery, Venice was "...exactly like a youthful dream." For Semmelweis that youthful dream embraced a sudden, complete silence, river-running streets with colorful gondolas slicing through, words in Italian drifting in. Streets of water on which edifices were suspended a thousand years. His eyes beheld wonders of art. If you were of a mind and heart for romance, there was no place on earth more amenable than Venice. The two friends listened to barcarolles on misty evenings on the Lido. Pull up slowly in a gondola to the church of Santa Maria della Salute, step off and enter this magnificent church and stand in front of a Titian and look up and marvel at the size, larger than life, and craftsmanship. It's said that Semmelweis took notes in museums and palaces that were soon lost. His relationship to paper and ink was not a very profitable able one. It's also said that he read ten books about Venice, at night, by candlelight. He is rapt before an open book, lit by gaslight, gleaming canal out his window. And he drags a tired Lajos everywhere: in gondolas, on foot, in carriages, by day and by night. The gondoliers are going too slow. Semmelweis takes over the steering, exhilarated, through the narrowest of canals. Lajos and the gondolier sit facing him, smiling.

Dr. Jacob Kolletchka

His destiny was barely a step ahead. Whether he desired it or not, was aware of it or not, his major place in the history of science and medicine pursues him, hounds him.—A.V.

Arrived back in Vienna in late March 1847, Semmelweis barely had time to settle into his quarters when tragic news greets him like a thunderbolt. His good friend and colleague Dr. Jacob Kolletschka died the day before.

Life often seems in a hurry. The way one major event, often a travesty, is followed by a completely different one, in complete disregard to rhythm and logic. Semmelweis wrote about this time:

"I was still under the influence of Venice and its attractions, thrilling to the artistic emotions I had felt during those two months I passed in the midst of those incomparable wonders when I heard about the death of poor Kolletschka. It put me in a state of extreme sensitivity…"

Poor Jakob Kolletschka was performing an autopsy for legal purposes, suddenly, a student's knife slips and accidentally pricks Kolletschka's finger. In the days that followed, he contracted lymphangitis and phlebitis in the upper extremity [inflammation of the lymphatic vessel and of the veins]. A metastasis formed in one of poor Kolletschka's eyes, and he died a few days later of bilateral pleurisy, pericarditis, and meningitis. The images surrounding Kolletschka's disease haunt Semmelweis day and night. A whirlwind of bells, staring eyes, Kolletchka hovering over a corpse, garbled words, student faces wide and still, a slipped knife, fount of blood…a wound opens, bleeds….Later on that early spring night, Semmelweis reads and re-reads his colleague's autopsy report. Organs and tissues permeated with pus and abnormalities exactly like those of women who die of puerperal fever, and sometimes their babies. Semmelweis himself is the best source of this Eurika, though tragic, moment:

"Totally shattered, I brooded over the case with intense emotion until suddenly a thought crossed my mind. At once it became clear to me that childbed fever, the fatal sickness of the newborn and the disease of Professor Kolletschka, were one and the same, because they consist pathologically of the same anatomic changes. If, therefore, in the case of Professor Kolletschka, general sepsis [contamination of the blood] arose from the inoculation of cadaver particles, then puerperal fever must originate from the same source. Now it was only necessary to decide from where and by what means the putrid cadaver particles were introduced into the delivery cases. The fact of the matter is that, as I had discovered prior to my dismissal, the transmitting source of those cadaver particles was found in the hands of the students and attending physicians." Semmelweis concludes: "Cadaveric particles were carried on the hands of students and attending physicians' fresh from their work in the autopsy room of examining the bodies of new mothers recently deceased of puerperal fever. Soap and water were available to wash the hands but it was not done systematically, since there was no real reason to do so. There was also no reason to change clothes. Then the medical students and attending physicians carried these hand-inundated infected cadaveric particles and introduced them into the expectant mothers' external genitalia, vagina and cervix. In turn, these particles were absorbed into the bloodstream and lymphatic channels and carried to organs and tissues. Transmission could also occur to the fetus whose vessels and those of the mother were still connected through the placenta. A particularly fertile site for cadaveric particle absorption in the post-partum mother was through the denuded area left vacant by the placenta."

Suppose, reasoned Semmelweis, "cadaverous particles adhering to the hands caused the same disease among maternity patients that cadaverous particles adhering to the student's knife caused in Kolletchka. Then, if those particles are destroyed chemically so that during examinations women are touched by disinfected fingers and not cadaverous particles, childbed fever had to be reduced."

Reflecting on his momentous discovery, Semmelweis understated it this way, definitively once and for all time to come—"Puerperal fever is nothing more than cadaveric poisoning."

Hands, human hands. From the time of Hippocrates to the present moment of medical annals in maternity hospitals around the world, Ignaz Semmelweis determines that the germs that lead to the puerperal scourge, the Fever that had killed so many over the millennia, were carried on the hands.

The way Semmelweis pursued his Destiny and his Destiny pursued him, Joseph Skoda kept a close eye on his protégée. Move Semmelweis to a secure, free-to-work position. Though Professor Bartsch did not need another assistant in the Second clinic, Dr. Skoda used his influence in persuading Bartsch to accept Semmelweis as Provisional Assistant. Semmelweis's work in Vienna was always so tenuous, always so important. His set-ups of pitchers and bowls of solutions of chlorine taken down when Klein had dismissed him were re-assembled and placed in Dissection and at the entrance and exits of the clinics. Johann Klein's clinic, too? The Director faced a choice. Refuse the hand washings or install them and prove Semmelweis wrong. He chose to install. Now every student and every examining physician whether or not he performed a dissection was made to carefully disinfect his hands with the chloride solution in the washstands found at the entrances and exits of the lying-in wards. Again, Semmelweis waits for results. One feels results in the throat. In the first full year of Semmelweis's program of sanitization, the puerperal death rate in the First Clinic was 1.2%; in the Second, 1.3%. Also, sequential deaths ceased.

History is made. Semmelweis had discovered the causes and means of prevention of a disease that had flourished for thousands of years, killing countless young new mothers and their babies.

Publish or Perish

"The results must speak for themselves."—Dr. I. P. Semmelweis

His findings and methods had to be legitimized, supported scientifically, through experiments and publications in recognized medical journals and publishers. Semmelweis may have understood this but it did not help him realize it. Student Semmelweis had studied the pioneering books of Drs. Leon Auenbrügger on percussion and Jean Corvisart's on the human heart. Drs. Joseph Skoda and Karl Rokitansky had recently published monographs on Diagnostics and Pathology. Semmelweis had to do the same. Publish, present papers which were also published, and perform lab experiments and publish those results, too.

The march of history establishes canon in diverse fields. From the year of his discovery 1847 to the end of his life, Semmelweis *was* the singular canon in Obstetrics. He was compelled at one and the same time to be researcher, scholar and practitioner. He was comfortable in the latter role. He was a brilliant, idiosyncratic scholar. He hated to speak and, more so, to write. There's something else Semmelweis may not have been aware of. Klein was waiting, crouched in the dark corner of malice and envy, for a misstep. Even those who cowed to the

Director and those who had maltreated personnel of the First Clinic, both sectors had the fallback position of saying that since Semmelweis could not prove his theory by means of the above, his work was no more legitimate than saying childbed fever was caused by a shift in atmospheric winds or by old walls in a state of disrepair.

How happy those women who came to the First Clinic must have been now that they had a good chance of seeing how their children would turn out.

The colleagues who watched and stood side by side with Semmelweis could relay the step-by step logic that had given rise to his conclusions. These men banded together. They recognized Semmelweis's vulnerabilities and believed in the accuracy of his findings. These great physicians, in addition to Skoda and Rokitansky, included Dr. Ferdinand Hebra.

Dr. Ferdinand Hebra

Ferdinand Hebra, regarded as the founder of the field of Dermatology, devoted time and energy in support of Semmelweis's work, realizing, perhaps, that saving women's lives was more of a priority than relieving a patient of an itch. Hebra and Semmelweis became fast friends. Hebra has been described as a sensitive man, capable of sarcasm and a sense of humor. Similar to Semmelweis. Later on, Hebra would trust Semmelweis with caring for his wife and delivering their child while wearing the National Guard uniform of wide-brim hat festooned with large, waving plume. Hebra would become famous for claiming that Semmelweis's work had a practical significance comparable to that of Edward Jenner's introduction of cowpox inoculations to prevent smallpox. Hebra picked up the slack caused by Semmelweis's disdain for writing by publishing articles in the December 1847 and April 1848 issues of the Viennese medical journal *Zeitschrift der k.k. Gesellschaft er Ärzte zu Wien*. It was the first public notice of the findings of Dr. Ignaz Semmelweis. Here is an excerpt:

"...the disease [childbed fever] is, in most cases, nothing other than an infection from corpses. To test this opinion, an ordinance was adopted in the labor rooms of the Obstetrical Clinics that everyone who examined patients must first wash in an aqueous solution of chloride of lime. The results were astonishingly successful. During April and May [1847] before this measure had been adopted, for each 100 births there were over 18 deaths. In the following months, and including 26 November, of 1,547 births there were 2.45 deaths...Dr. Semmelweis believes himself able to prove that first, in September, through negligent washing by a few students occupied with anatomy, several patients died. Second, in October through frequent examinations of a patient with discharging medullary carcinoma of the uterus, after which washings were not observed; and third, through the presence of a patient with a discharging leg wound--many patients present became infected at the same time. Therefore, the transfer of exuding ichor from living organisms can cause puerperal fever...We request the directors of all maternity clinics to report their confirming or disconfirming evidence."

Through the Post

Burning the midnight oil, Semmelweis and Hebra sit side by side and write letters by hand to the major obstetricians in Europe, detailing Semmelweis's work, requesting that they follow his prescription and then, confirming or disconfirming, inform them of results. In this way, these colleagues resembled the medieval troubadour poets who wrote poems on the subject of love and then sent them on their way on horseback and ship to other poets, requesting their responses. Perhaps the most famous such call and response can be found in Dante Alighieri's *A New Life,* wherein the great medieval poet wrote about a dream: in a fiery cloud his muse Beatrice is asleep sprawled in the arms of Love, loosely wrapped in a blood-red cloth, and Love holds a fiery object in his hand. "Behold your heart!" exclaims Love, and then he awakens Beatrice and urges her to eat the heart in his hand, the dreamer's heart, which, after some hesitation, she does. Then Dante sends his dream-poem "To every captive soul and gentle heart." Many artists replied, among them the first of Dante's friends, Guido Cavalcanti, who replied: "In my opinion you saw all that is of worth."

Semmelweis saw all that is of worth in women.

Letterboxes, postage stamps, telegraph stations and mail delivery by rail had recently come into use. These correspondences of great import, procedures and results of one Dr. Ignaz Semmelweis, were carried by mail-coaches, pulled by horses. They were delivered to Drs. Tilanus in Amsterdam, Simpson in Edinburg, Schmidt in Berlin, Scanzoni in Würtsburg, Seyfert in Prague.

Ferdinand Hebra confessed to a colleague:

"We could not doubt that, far from local jealousies and malice, we were going to receive the complete approval of those who could not fail to find Semmelweis's experiments completely conclusive."

Rabbits

While waiting for feedback, Semmelweis enlisted Dr. Georg Marie Lautner to join him in a series of nine experiments on rabbits. Lautner was a friend and also a protégé of Rokitansky's and an active member of the progressive young faculty. Semmelweis and Lautner collected the rabbits and placed them in cages. A fiction writer would most likely gather research on the availability of rabbits for research, any animal rights activists at the time, whether other departments used rabbits for research, plus the look and feel and set-up of the imperial hospital's lab. Cold metal, test tubes, gas lamps. In a few years, mid-1850s, Robert Bunson would introduce the Bunson burner in a laboratory in Germany. Our researchers in shirts with their sleeves rolled up, first in the Dead House where the air is cold, stale and reeking, saturate their brushes with decayed discharge taken from the abdomens of those new mothers recently dead of puerperal fever. Picture a woman's corpse lying there. The doctors push on, surrounded by unimaginable tragedy. Then they go over to the lab and insert such infected brushes into the vagina and uterus of three postpartum rabbits. All three died. Then take the three rabbit corpses over to Dissection. Findings are precisely the same as those found in the cadavers.

Then they vary their experiments. Back to Autopsy and the remains of a half-dozen men, one who had died of malnutrition, and take blood. They take chest fluid and peritoneal fluid from a victim of tuberculosis. Peritoneal fluid from a man who had died of typhus. They extract pus from an abscess between the ribs of a man who had died of cholera. Then the researchers inject these different fluids in the post-partum rabbits. These were their findings: The rabbit inoculated with chest and peritoneal fluids remained healthy. The rabbit inoculated with infected chest fluid from a man dead of typhus died but with findings not those of childbed fever. The rabbit injected with pus from the abscess between the ribs of a cholera victim remained healthy. Three inoculated rabbits died from causes not characteristic of puerperal fever. Semmelweis went on to over-read his findings. He declared: "The changes found in the rabbit cadavers are the same as appear in human bodies as a result of puerperal diseases." This assessment was true only of the first three inoculated rabbits. Six did not support the total body of his experiments. Semmelweis's experiments with rabbits would serve him little purpose.

The Reception

At this point in the lifework of Ignaz Semmelweis in the annals of science and medicine, one could say that it was done. He'd discovered the causes and means of prevention of puerperal fever. His work was saving the lives of countless women in childbirth and was disseminated to obstetricians around the world. Now it was a question of what they would make of it. It had certainly been enough for Dr. Destouches in his medical school monograph. Dr. Semmelweis's life could have ended right now. The great Hungarian physician's cure was tantamount to finding a cure for cancer and now he would discover to his woe the kind of music fellow obstetricians, science's status quo and the ilk of Klein would make him dance to. And a danse macabre it would be.

What more could Semmelweis do than offer the entirety of his life, his own mortal self?

After the case of the woman in the First Clinic erroneously diagnosed as pregnant and then Semmelweis correctly re-diagnosed her with cervical cancer, he went straightaway, without washing his hands with his own solution, to examining pregnant women--and they died soon thereafter. He managed to write with great pain:

"Because of my convictions, I must here confess that God only knows the number of patients who have gone to their graves prematurely by my fault. I have handled cadavers extensively, more than most *accoucheurs*. If I say the same of another physician, it is only to bring to light a truth, which was unknown for many centuries with direful results for the human race. As painful and depressing,

136

indeed, as such an acknowledgment is, still the remedy does not lie in concealment and this misfortune should not persist forever, for the truth must be made known to all concerned."

Responses begin coming in. Excited, hands rapid and trembling, Drs. Semmelweis, Ferdinand Hebra and Joseph Skoda open letters and read one and then another.

Recurring:

"We attending physicians, our hands, even our shirtsleeves, he is saying, have come into contact with this decayed animal matter in autopsy and then carried upon our person while examining women in term...."How dare this Jewish Hungarian Assistant declare that we physicians, appointed by the Austrian Minister of Education, most of us tenured before Semmelweis was born, are the cause of the spread of puerperal fever. We have been, and remain, powerless in the face of the scourge."

If Semmelweis's theories were proven true, they could be called assassins and, who knew, possibly lose their heads.

Wow! News from England's most prominent obstetrician, Dr. James Simpson:

"British obstetrical literature must be totally unknown in Vienna or Semmelweis would have known that the British have long regarded childbed fever as contagious…"

Semmelweis begins his unfortunate practice of lashing back:

"Every corpse, regardless of the disease that caused death, can bring about childbed fever. It follows that childbed fever is not a contagious disease. It is, rather, a pyemia such as is brought on in experiments on animals."

From Amsterdam, Dr. Christian Bernard Tilanus:

"Yes, cadaver poisoning appears to be a factor in transmission, but periodic instances of epidemics indicate that atmospheric influence is also involved. Therefore, I did not see any reason for introducing hand washing in my clinic."

How many new mothers were dying unnecessarily in Tilanus' clinic in Amsterdam?

Positive response from Dr. Gustav Adolph Michaelis of Kiel. And more—he has forwarded details of Semmelweis' discoveries to his colleague Karl Levy in Copenhagen.

Await Levy's response which, in time, is:

"Chlorine washings are needed but the amount of infective matter or vapor secluded around the fingernails could not be enough to kill a patient."

For his part, Dr. Hebra extends their work to addressing the group of obstetricians skeptical that cadaveric poisoning is not the sole cause of childbed fever. He details the two cases of the patient with infected knee attended by nurses who then, with unwashed hands, attended women in labor who died a few days thereafter. And second, the case of the woman originally misdiagnosed as pregnant whom Semmelweis went on to diagnose properly with cancer and then he himself, with unwashed hands, went on to deliver women who died several days later. These two separate etiologies were ignored or skipped over. The juxtaposition of images of new mothers momentarily joyous giving birth and the ravages of the disease that then grips them was, perhaps, too powerful for men to visualize, digest, sustain.

Friedrich Wilhelm Scanzoni and Josef Schmidt refused to accept blame. How many new mothers in their clinics in Würtsburg and Berlin were dying unnecessarily?

The race was on, pathetic Scanzoni in the vanguard, about who would get credit for curing puerperal fever.

Colleague Dr. Carl Haller: Schmidt has underreported maternity deaths in his Charité clinic in Berlin.

Semmelweis: True, there were 13 deaths out of 2,631 patients at his clinic over the past few years but 442 patients had been "transferred to other stations" as soon as the health of new mothers began to suffer.

Envy pursues Semmelweis unrelentingly. There was much more hidden support for his findings than recognized. His views were repeated by obstetricians without attribution. Many were embarrassed to admit to associating with a controversial, eccentric, impossibly difficult Assistant.

Dr. Charles Routh

In addition to letters and word-of-mouth, disseminate news of Semmelweis's theory and practice through in-person presentations. That was the idea--no, the mission—of young physician Charles Henry Felix Routh, a former student of Semmelweis's who had worked side-by-side with him throughout his experiments and saw and verified results. War was breaking out in Europe, South America, too. Monarchies were transforming to republics through the bloodshed of the finest young men and women of their generation, resistance to change stubborn, which Semmelweis's discoveries echoed in the field of Obstetrics. Routh's illustrious British family called him back home to London. He would use the opportunity to present a paper--"memoir," scientific papers were called then-- in the flesh, stand at the lectern in proud full body and voice at the annual meeting of the illustrious Royal Medical and Chirurgical society, composed of the finest obstetricians and gynecologists of the day. His presentation would erase all doubt and inform all hypocritical lack of understanding. Routh was called Semmelweis's first "apostle," as he lived to the end of the century and so witnessed the introduction of the compound microscope and the work of Louis Pasteur and still continued Semmelweis's practices well into the 20th century.

Young Routh climbs into his coach and four, destination London. He carries all proper documentation and clutches in a case against his breast, notes and documents for his talk. The journey by coach is long and rickety, more than 900 miles. Horses have to rest after 30 miles. Routh, eyed unknowingly by the other passengers, sits still, wearing a pensive, faraway look. This important physician was born in Valletta, Malta, on January 4th, 1822, fourteen years Semmelweis's junior, his father Sir Randolph Isham Routh, K.C.B, Knight Commander of the Bath, Commissary General in the British Army. In 1840, Charles Routh joined the Medical Faculty of University College and then went on to study in Paris, Prague and Vienna.

Out from a gray, wet London, Dr. Routh slogs up to his humble room, optimistic, exhilarated. Soon, the world will know about and practice Semmelweis' doctrine.

Back in Vienna, Semmelweis waits for his student's report, his heart out to him..

On rubbery legs, his heart pounding, Dr. Routh enters the great hall of the Medical Society of London. Out of the corner of his eye he can see that it rises and spreads out and up like that of a grand opera house. It is packed with bearded physicians all dressed in black.

He will read his presentation but has also committed it to memory, that which he had rehearsed in the rickety coach on the trip from Vienna to London, his notes dancing on his lap. After switching personnel in Vienna's two lying-in clinics, medical students in one just come from Dissection with midwives in the other, Dr. Semmelweis thus equalized respective mortality rates. He will look up and explain. The finger prick of the unfortunate Dr. Kolletschka and his autopsy report, which Dr. Semmelweis recognized as the same as that of new mothers who still today were lying in Autopsy rooms around the world. Details of the two cases: the woman misdiagnosed and the one with infected knee, from which Semmelweis showed that cadaveric poisoning is not the sole source of infection and transmission.

"My esteemed colleagues, Semmelweis has shown that puerperal fever is, in this way, a misnomer. Men, children—anyone--can contract childbed fever. Yes, students and attending physicians alike just like yourselves wash their hands with soap and water, but the hands still reek of contaminated particles too small to see. The ugly odiferous representation of disease inevitably transfers to your bloody hands. Washing of the hands with a solution of chloride of lime as recommended by Dr. Semmelweis eliminates infected exudations...." and so forth.

But then a Society member approaches Dr. Routh.

"You, personally, cannot give your paper, as you are not a member of our Royal Medical Society. Though one such member of your choice can deliver it."

"Uh, yes, Dr. Edward Murphy,* if you please."

Dr. Murphy had been one of his teachers and the one who inspired him with a zeal for obstetrics and gynecology.

Imagine how Routh must have felt? Come all that way, so much at stake...Semmelweis waiting, hoping. Routh's great heart kept beating fast while he watched and listened closely to Dr. Murphy present Semmelweis's work.

Dr. Murphy:

146

"Dr. Routh's paper is entitled 'On the Causes
of the Endemic Puerperal Fever of Vienna'. In
Vienna there was a midwives' clinic and a students'
clinic, the wards in the former were not so large nor
so airy as those in the latter, yet the mortality in the
wards where the students were instructed was
scandalous…ranging from 1 in 3 in their clinic to 1 in 9
in the midwives'….The real source is found in the
hands of the medical men in attendance contaminated
with cadaveric poisons, staff and students, who
diligently attended the numerous autopsies in the
adjacent Dead House. Then Semmelweis,
remembering how the midwife students made no
autopsies and worked on the phantom, put all
students in quarantine for a day after attending an
autopsy and directed all who worked in the students'
midwifery clinic to wash their hands in a solution of
chlorine prior to and after every examination made
on the living subject. The result of these
precautionary measures was that the number of

deaths at once fell to seven per month, or the usual average in the midwives' clinic…Michaelis, of Kiel, had for several months employed chlorinated lotions and had only lost one patient, although before that period the mortality was so great that he had been deliberating the closure of his hospital…."

Dr. Routh was pleased. Dr. Murphy had covered essential points. But then it was in the equivocal remarks afterwards from those in attendance that sank Routh's expansive heart.

Dr. Webster, Physician to the St. George's and St. James's Dispensary, stands:

"The Vienna hospital is situated in a damp position, and is ill-ventilated and unclean. The students also are anything but cleanly."

Dr. Murphy replies:

"The novel point in Routh's paper is the fact established by the author that puerperal fever was propagated by the students who had been recently examining dead bodies."

Then the Society's president, Dr. J. Moncrieff Arnott, asks, "Does Dr. Semmelweis's findings accord with the experience of the accoucheurs present, that is, that pupils from the dissection gave puerperal fever to their lying-in patients more frequently?"

A pause. Routh looks around, up, down…Silence. Not a voice.

Dr. Gregory, of the Small Pox Hospital, gets up and poses another question: "Why has puerperal fever been so prevalent in lying-in hospitals?" Dr. Copeland, Consulting Physician to Charlotte's Hospital: "I admit that the facts in Routh's paper are so convincing that obstetricians could scarcely doubt their accuracy. But, esteemed sirs, my experience is that matrons and midwives who did not examine bodies were not free from contamination." Routh squirms in his seat. The discussion is moving further and further away from the Truth.

D. Webster criticizes Routh for paying insufficient attention to the circumstances in Vienna:

"It is well known that Vienna is the most unhealthy place in Europe. Fever of a low type is very prevalent there. The hospital is situated in a damp position, and is ill-ventilated, and unclean. The students, also, are anything but cleanly."

Mr. C. Hewitt Moore, Surgeon to the Middlesex Hospital: "The amount of post-mortem examination going on in the Vienna University was remarkable. I saw as many as fifteen bodies lying for examination in a morning. The students and professors had their hands immersed in these corpses for hours--"

"Yes, go on," murmurs Routh to himself. Then—

Moore: "The city itself is insanitary and typhus {i.e., typhoid) is prevalent."

In conclusion, Dr. Marshall: "Take caution, my fellows, that ablution in chloride of lime is not absolutely trustworthy. I'd been examining a body, was called from thence to a labour but took the precaution of changing all my clothes and washed my hands in said solution of chloride of lime. My patient, however, was seized with puerperal fever, and the next day following three suffered from the same malady."

Afterwards, Routh, frantic, approaches President Moncrieff Arnott:

"Sir, may I make presentations to individual obstetricians?"

Pause. Slowly, eyes staring into Routh's soul, Moncrieff Arnott shakes his head.

Late, in the light of his gas lamp, devastated by "the inertia and the distain of the truth," Dr. Routh writes to Semmelweis:

"...I can say that the lecture was well-received, and that many of the most informed members testified that the evidence is conclusive. In particular, [John} Webster, [George A.] Copeland, and [Edward William] Murphy, all distinguished physicians, spoke most favorably."

Dr. Skoda's Lecture*

It was a lecture delivered by the illustrious Joseph Skoda that did about as much to support Semmelweis's claims as his experiments on rabbits.

Two months after Semmelweis concluded his experiments on rabbits, Joseph Skoda delivered a major lecture to the Vienna Academy of Sciences, the most prestigious scientific organization in Austria. Skoda's lecture was then published in the organization's journal, which was distributed far and wide. Now all could read how Skoda listed the maternity hospitals with the highest mortality rates and suggested that especially these should take notice of Semmelweis's work and certainly establish his prescribed hand-washings. Highlighted was the maternity hospital in Würtzburg, where 27 out of 102 new mothers had died during that year (26.5%), and the lying-in clinic in Prague. Skoda *named* the professors of obstetrics: Friedrich Wilhelm Scanzoni and Bernhard Seyfert.* These are the obstetricians who were not using Semmelweis's prophylaxis of hand-washing of chloride of lime. These are the men who had killed at least fifty new mothers. This high rate, Skoda had the audacity to say, stemmed for the need in a small maternity clinic like Würtzburg's for every patient to be used as teaching material, while at Vienna General, hundreds of patients are not so used and, therefore, not a source of infection. Suddenly, due to this upstart Assistant Semmelweis, they, Scanzoni and Seyfert, had gone from blameless and powerless in the face of the puerperal scourge to responsible and guilty.

Both physicians denied categorically that cadaveric poisoning caused childbed fever at *their* clinic. And they had instituted chloride washings without a significant reduction in the death rate. Scanzoni seized the opportunity to put forward his own theory on the etiology of childbed fever: "…changes in blood constitution, carried by cosmotelluric influences. By no means is the wound of the uterus represented by the placental site the real cause of origin of the puerperal fever."

Wilhelm Scanzoni joins Johann Klein as a principal unrelenting, inconsolable detractor of Semmelweis's program. Fourteen years after Skoda's call out, Semmelweis wrote: "…it might have occurred to Scanzoni that precisely these weighty arguments deterred his students from washing as conscientiously as necessary. As a rule, the fingertips were dipped once into a dark liquid that had been used for the same purpose for several days…many of the students discontinued even this operation and washed with plain water."

More and more new mothers went on to die. And then the petty jealousies of men were inconvenienced by revolution.

Revolution

The revolution caused by Semmelweis' findings on the scientific front coincided and mirrored revolutions of a political nature in the major capitals of Europe and as far away as South America. Monarchies were about to topple in favor of republics. The blood of patriots began to spill on the fields of battle, the way new mothers' blood spilled on bed sheets of maternity clinics. In medicine there were Semmelweis, Skoda, Hebra, Haller, Michaelis, Rokintansky. In war, in Hungary, Kossuth and in Rome, fighting under Garibaldi, the poet warrior Mameli, Luciano Manara, the Cairoli brothers, the American journalist Margaret Fuller and Anita Garibaldi.

The field of obstetrics as Semmelweis knew it was beset with as much blood and sacrifice as the streets of Rome during the War of the Roman Republic of 1848. Healthy women swept the streets so that the horses could have surer footing. Surviving 14-year-old boys fought with muskets side by side with guerilla fighters. The best of their generation gave their lives to medicine and the fight for democratic principles.

Skoda, Garibaldi, Rokitansly, Mazzini, Hebra, Kossuth, Semmelweis—they grew and came of age during the aftermath of the Congress of Vienna, from 1820 to 1848. The forces of progress embodied in men such as these grew potent in the face of extreme repression and wide-spread epidemics. Political revolution and the truth of medicine's etiologies and prophylaxes were not overnight affairs. They aged and bore fruit as the century wore on.

The Austrian empire found itself fighting on several fronts: Vienna, Budapest, Rome. The empire used the majority of its army under Field Marshal Radetsky against the revolutionaries in Rome who had established a Republic, ruled by Giuseppe Mazzini and General Giuseppe Garibaldi. Pope Pius IX had fled to the Neapolitan Kingdom disguised as a page. The papacy and its temporal powers, lands and army, had to be restored in Rome at all cost. Vienna could not rule its subjects without a puppet pope to worship not only in the Eternal City but around the world. The Divine Right of Kings required a temporal Divinity. Without a pope in Rome, there would be no Holy Roman Empire or Emperor, and that would augur the end of the Austrian Empire.

The plight of women in childbirth was the least of Austria's worries. The crown shut down Vienna Hospital's maternity clinics. Dissecting rooms and lying-in clinics were empty, bloodless.

During the month of March 1848, both lying-in clinics did not report a single new mother dead of puerperal fever. Semmelweis would use this statistic as further proof that the interference of the human agency was the main cause of puerperal fever.

Revolutionary Semmelweis

Hungary is, in a word, in a state of WAR against the Hapsburg dynasty, a war of legitimate defense, by which alone it can ever regain independence and freedom....The power that is supported by force alone will have cause oft to tremble.—Lajos Kossuth

Semmelweis's active participation in revolutionary activities in Vienna and Hungary is subsumed to his career in medicine. Much less is known, necessarily. Reasons could be that he survived his revolutionary days and, after uprisings were put down, returned to his career in Vienna, unlike his brothers who had to go into hiding. Also because, unlike in Italy and in his clinics, upheavals were bloodless, and also Semmelweis the Patriot displayed the upbeat aspect of his character, as he'd had in Venice. He was filled with hope for a more democratic Austria, for a nation's soul commensurate to the work he was doing in behalf of women's and children's health. Fortunately for himself and other colleagues and students, uprisings close to and inside, Vienna were relatively bloodless, taking the form more of protests than armed fighting, like in Rome. Vienna's Court officers fled. Sixty thousand university students and progressive faculty formed the Academic Legion. In his *Reminiscences*, Carl Schurz describes the revolutionaries' uniform:

> "... black felt hats with ostrich plumes; blue coats with lack shining buttons; tricolored, black-red-gold sashes; bright steel-handled swords; light-gray trousers; and silver-gray cloaks lined with scarlet.

They looked like a troop of
knights of old."

Students and faculty took to the streets,
marched and shouted slogans, banners waving:
"*Lehrfreiheit und Lernfreiheit!*" "Freedom of teaching
and freedom of learning." "No more serfdom.
"Freedom of the Press." "The right to assemble."

Semmelweis and his brothers József and
Fülöp put up barricades along *Kaerntner* and
Ringstrasse. Marching, waving his banner,
Semmelweis joined the chorus of the recently
published Hungarian anthem.* There was dancing in
Buda's streets. His colleague Dr. Brücke would
write:

"Ein flotter Tänzer!" "Can he dance."

A dancing Semmelweis! For the first time in
years, the image of a dead new mother was not
directly before his eyes. He associated with artists
and politicians. He took his first riding lesson and
was seen on horseback every morning amid

Budapest's high society. He was a cultivated, entertaining physician. In the middle of winter, he learned to swim and, like the men and women of Polar Bear Clubs, a crowd cheered as he dove into icy waters. He squandered his inheritance of two thousand crowns, equivalent today to several hundred dollars. Dr. L.F. Destouches is inconsolable in regards to Semmelweis having a semblance of a normal life:

"Society and dancing set him on his way toward the feminine. He was wasting what little time was left to him."

Had he found a lady friend in his war-torn country?

With brothers József and Fülöp in hiding, Semmelweis returned to the hospital and his work in Vienna.

Continuum

The year 1848 waned and uprisings put down, and in their wake Vienna Imperial's lying-in clinics re-opened and faculty and students returned and pregnant women came to give birth, with the result that, thanks to Semmelweis's program of prophylaxis, the majority lived to see their children survive. Not only had the medical school faculty achieved autonomy through mainly the students' insurrection, but also many of the old, reactionary guard were forced into retirement, knowing that over the years, in the lying in-clinics of one of the most prestigious teaching hospitals in the world, they had contributed to the deaths of hundreds upon hundreds of new mothers and days-old babies.

Semmelweis continued to wear his Academic Legion uniform while he lectured
and made his rounds. His show of stubborn pride and patriotic fervor did not go
unnoticed, especially by Johann Klein, who exhibited equal fervor by using his influence

to remain Clinic director and block Semmelweis.

The revolution brought the pioneering group of physicians closer in that they understood Semmelweis's reluctance to write and publish and conduct further lab experiments. Records had been lost during the tumult of revolution. And so the ever astute Joseph Skoda, recognized now as the preeminent physician in Austria, proposed to the faculty at large that a commission be established to study and evaluate Semmelweis's *Lehr*. His historic findings would be re-established, re-affirmed in this new context of peace and a stronger medical establishment.

The faculty agreed. Klein did not. He blocked it. A state-sponsored commission
could possibly reveal the truth.

But Joseph Skoda persevered. He arranged to give a second lecture to the members of the Vienna Academy of Science. In this new context of peace and a stronger faculty...louder, more prominent voices to shout Semmelweis's news. Like his first unfortunate lecture during which he named names, this one would also be published but translated and read by obstetricians around the world.

Skoda goes to Records and finds records piled floor-to-ceiling of three quarters of a century and maternity death rates since the early 1840s.

Skoda: September, October...here we are...

But this month's record was missing. A void.... Klein had calculated correctly. He had prepared, too. Bar access to the current low death rate and have Skoda go on to rely on Semmelweis himself for historical information and records. Disaster! But Klein did not have time to confiscate the previous month's statistics, which marked a decrease in the death rate.

Skoda decided to use that stat and then he arranged a tête-à-tête with Semmelweis to go over his findings and actions.

Head bowed, the great senior physician is patient, listens to Semmelweis's step-by-step to his discoveries, then Skoda writes more or less the same information as his first lecture, this one without naming names.

How did Semmelweis feel having his mentor speak in his behalf? Much the same way as the young, enthusiastic Dr. Routh had felt when he was not allowed to deliver his prepared lecture in London. But this was slightly different. Semmelweis was about to listen to a prominent someone else sing his song.

On the evening of October 18, 1849, Skoda gives his talk. The hall is packed, rows of physicians dressed in black with beards, heads forward, wide-eyed, listening intently. Skoda carefully, meticulously presents the evolution of Semmelweis's *Lehr:* his brilliant observation of the major difference under their nose of medical students of the First Clinic versus midwives of the Second, switching them, then his finding that death followed the students. Going from Dissection to Examinations and Delivery with washings of soap and water. The tragic accident and death of Professor Kolletchka. Similarities in autopsy reports....Program of systematic hand washings with solutions of chloride of lime. The plummeting death rate. Certainly, Skoda spoke about the two cases that showed that the source of puerperal fever was not solely the transfer of cadaveric particles.

"Are we not privileged, gentlemen, that it will be known for all time that the

myriad causes and modes of prevention of a disease that has plagued humanity for

thousands of years were discovered in our midst, in our hospital, by one of our colleagues..."

"Once again those who heard Skoda's talk came away with the wrong impression."—Dr. Sherwin Nuland

That is, that cadaveric particles were the sole cause of puerperal fever.

Skoda's lecture was once again published in the Science Academy's journal. Subsequently, Semmelweis was elected as a member. He had gained a modicum of prestige. Being a voted member of the prestigious Academy and, at the same time, having his work largely misunderstood could not have pleased him. Most likely vexed him, as did the increasing number of negative comments.

Swan Song

It was spring again, this time in 1849, and edelweiss were in bloom and Semmelweis's tenure of two-year assistantship ended. He requested an extension of two more years. Such an extension had been granted to his predecessor, Dr. Breit, as it also had to his colleague in the Second Clinic, Dr. Franz Zipfl. But Dr. Carl Braun also applied for the position, most likely at Klein's invitation.

Semmelweis's application was supported by Drs. Skoda and Rokitansky and most of the medical faculty, but Klein chose Braun. Semmelweis was obliged to leave the obstetrical clinic when his term expired on March 20, 1849.

That day, Semmelweis petitioned the Viennese authorities to be made docent of obstetrics. A docent was a private lecturer who taught students and also had access to some university facilities. At first, because of Klein's opposition, Semmelweis's petition

was denied. He then appealed to the dean, who could have overruled Klein's refusal.

In the meantime, Klein submitted to this anonymous dean that Semmelweis's behavior

was autocratic and thereby detrimental in the way he demanded that all students,

staff and physicians wash their hands with a chloride solution before examining patients. Corroboration of this outrage was given by Dr. Anton Rosas, professor of ophthalmology, a neutral field. Semmelweis had to be replaced in order to relieve the adverse effects of the animosity between himself and Semmelweis. This was one, undeniable truth espoused by Dr. Johann Klein. The latter was a man who had done absolutely nothing in his life and career to save one new mother, while Semmelweis devoted the whole of his in doing so, and succeeded.

The dean ruled against Semmelweis. Clinical evidence in support of the drastically lowered death rate of new mothers had not factored in to his decision.

Then he applied for a position called *Privatdozent* in midwifery. He would establish a private practice and, at the same time, teach in the medical school. He waited for an answer.

In the meantime, he agreed to give a series of talks to the Medical Society of Vienna. It would be his first public presentation of his work. Professor

Karl von Rokitansky was society president, so he felt somewhat secure. Of course, supportive colleagues Skoda, Hebra, Routh and Markusovszky would attend. This series of talks was the way Semmelweis chose for his great colleagues to remember him. His presence. His voice. His work. His legacy. And that is what happened.

On a lovely early spring of May 15, 1850-- three years after discovering the causes of childbed fever and its means of prevention—Semmelweis approaches the lectern. How is he dressed? What does he sound like?

"He is said to have handled himself well during the talk and the ensuing question and answer period."—Dr. Sherwin Nuland

In a photograph* taken in 1853 of the collegium the Vienna Medical School, of the fifteen professors in attendance, nine were active in teaching, speaking and writing about the *Lehr*.

He must have been engaging, for he was invited back to speak, not once but twice.

His talk one month later centered around responses to critics, a sorry task which, in time, would transform to a self-destructive obsession. That which he had discovered saved life upon life, everywhere. He himself named names. News of Semmelweis's public critical response to him must have reached Dr. Wilhelm Scanzoni in Würtzburg, fueling the fire of his venomous opposition. The more Semmelweis's work spread in a positive manner, the deeper Scanzoni, and scores of other obstetricians, felt self-indicted. Scanzoni's disdain, and fear, went so far as advising his students to sabotage the very act of washing their hands with solutions of chloride. Semmelweis received proof of this from colleague George Martius, who wrote to him:

"…I saw with my own eyes that normally nothing like a true washing was involved. As a rule the fingers were dipped once into a dark liquid that had been used for the same purpose for several days…many students discontinued even this operation and washed with soap and water."

Semmelweis gave his third and final talk one month later, on July 15, 1849.

Dr. Theodore Helm stood up and pointed out the differences between Semmelweis's *Lehr* and the English contagionists, which Skoda and Hebra had also highlighted in their talks. Then, to Johann Klein's horror, Dr. Johann Chiari stood up and said that he had been the great innovator's teacher of obstetrics upon his graduation, and had witnessed the *Lehr* develop, step by step, and had washed his hands in the first washstands containing a solution of chloride of lime, and had waited and then seen the incontrovertible decline in deaths.

Johann Klein must have paled. Dr. Chiari had married his daughter. Chiari was his son-in-law. How did Mrs. Chiari fare amid this tension?

Chiari regarded it as a matter of conscience that he publish his observations.

But Semmelweis did not submit his lectures for formal publication. His hatred of the writing process extended to publishing his lectures. To seeing words in print, especially of his own making. Efficient opponent Dr. Eduard Lumpe had his dissenting remarks published in full.

What Semmelweis did was reduce his talks to abstracts in the medical society's minutes. But not everyone read minutes. And those who did, once again, were left without a true understanding of his program.

For every step Semmelweis took forward, life pushed back two.

On March 20, 1849, at the age of 31, after being denied renewed tenure in Klein's maternity ward, Semmelweis petitioned Viennese authorities for the position of private docent of obstetrics. Such a docent was a private lecturer who also had access to university facilities and was paid by the students themselves. A tutor with privileges. Again, Klein blocked the appointment. Skoda moved for the appointment of a committee of professors to inquire and prepare statistics, including a table to show the comparative results in cases of street-births. Klein protested. He obtained the interference of the Minister of Education. Semmelweis reapplied and waited a year for an answer. Months, sometimes years pass in the life of Ignaz Semmelweis, undocumented. Per Skoda's urging, Semmelweis conducted more experiments on rabbits.

In the laboratory he brushes with blood and other fluids from human corpses, of which, apparently, there never was a lack, the genitals of newly delivered rabbits. The majority of rabbits died. Dissection revealed remains similar to those found in victims of childbed fever. This further research on rabbits did not abet or diminish his career.

After a wait of eight months, his application for *Privatdozent* was finally approved at a faculty meeting held in March 1850. It appeared that his plan of establishing a private practice in Vienna and teaching in the medical school was approaching fruition. His approved application was forwarded to the Ministry of Education, along with the faculty's recommendation that Semmelweis be exempted from the ministry's outdated rule that a *Privatdozent* teach using "the phantom," the female anatomical model, instead of a real cadaver. The ministry accepted the faculty's recommendation. But, suddenly, someone with influence—who could it have been?--intervened. With the result that Semmelweis's appointment's directive in regard to "the phantom" was changed. His course announcement for the winter session 1850-'51 reads:

"Lectures on midwifery with practical demonstrations on the phantom five times a week by Dozent Ignác Semmelweis."

Insulted, the proverbial last straw was laid upon his weighted shoulders, Dr. Semmelweis hastily packed a few things in the dead of night. He stole away, like a phantom himself. He would never return to Vienna, willingly.

PART V: BUDAPEST

Hungry was regularly and completely despoiled...for the spirit, it was a night which descended from 1849 until 1867.—Dr. L.F. Destouches

Night descended for Semmelweis in a home country where famine prevailed, an ideal condition for Austria together with Russia to drive out the occupying Croats and establish a military dictatorship. Metternich had fled Vienna, and the Hungarian Diet, led by Lajos Kossuth, attempted in vain to establish Magyar as Hungary's official language, which was as foreign to Semmelweis almost as much as Latin and German. At the same time, Semmelweis had no prospects, little money and, as it turned out, little time.

The dictatorship intruded upon university affairs. Dr. János Balassa, professor of surgery and provost of the University of Budapest, was thrown into jail. Dr. Bujatz, editor of the medical gazette, fled to Switzerland. One medical society was allowed to convene once a month, under the surveillance of a police superintendant.

"We can no longer see each other, no one can keep up to date with similar work of peers, no experiments get duplicated. We are living in the shadows."—Dr. Peter Kotanyi.

Everywhere Semmelweis turned he encountered shadows. Still, women continued to give birth, those of that supervising police officer's wife and daughters, as well as the women of Professor Kotanyi's family. The families of decorated despots showered their babies with equal hope of good health.

Semmelweis was invited to meet with a number of physicians. He had achieved some notoriety in Vienna. His name was synonymous with childbed fever. But the majority voiced objections to his theory of causality. At that very moment, an epidemic of childbed fever was raging in their local maternity ward of St. Rochus's hospital, he was told. Since it was not a teaching hospital, not a single hand, washed or otherwise, of a male student or attending physician went from dissecting the corpse of a new mother, or of anyone for that matter, to examining and delivering a prospective mother.

Prominent obstetricians Eduard von Siebold of Göttingen and Bernhard Sigismund Schultze of Jena visited him. Perhaps he took the visiting professors with him after this meeting of physicians to investigate the so-called epidemic at the 675-bed St. Rocha's Hospital.

That odor of decaying organic matter greets them. The odor of women dying shadowed Semmelweis from his first day in Vienna through his years in Budapest to his last days in Vienna again.

Up three flights to St. Rochus's maternity ward, which consisted of a labor room and two maternity rooms. The ward was staffed by three medical and two surgical head physicians. One new mother had just died of childbed fever, one was in its death throes, and four others in its first stages. The obstetrical ward was assigned to the surgical ward. It lacked a coroner, so that the various division physicians performed autopsies and then, without washing their hands with solutions of chloride, examined women in the maternity ward. True, as the physicians of the night before had claimed, no students examined the pregnant women with contaminated hands—but the versatile chief physician had. Semmelweis would write:

"In the maternity ward of St. Rochus, the great mortality of maternity patients is explained by the fact that the head surgeon was simultaneously the head obstetrician. The mortality rate in this hospital depended on decaying matter generated by the sick.... For two years, the excessive mortality rate was caused by decaying matter from the third source(other than cadaveric poisoning)."

St. Rochus, or Roch, or Rocco, is known for healing victims of the "plague," which meant *any* epidemic. Dr Ignaz Semmelweis is known as savior of women in childbirth, any woman. Both men were born into well-to-do families. Rochus's father was governor of the southern French town of Montpelier in the south of France. It was a miracle that Rochus was even born in the first place, as his mother was deemed barren. But then she prayed to the Virgin Mary, and a boy was born to the noble woman with a red cross on his chest. As he grew, so did the red cross. It was unlikely, if not a miracle, that Ignaz Philipp would distinguish himself from his eight siblings and pursue the path of a physician rather than merchant like his father and brothers. Upon his father's death, Rochus gave away everything and assumed the life of a mendicant pilgrim, traveling down through Italy and into Rome. A plague was raging. Rochus prayed. Time and again, he made the sign of the cross on the foreheads of the sick and dying. The cardinal of Angleria was cured after Rochus made the sign of the cross on *his* forehead, and the cross remained. How many thousands of women had Semmelweis touched in a positive manner throughout his lifetime of work? Rochus fell ill himself in the Italian town of Piacenza and was expelled, perhaps for the same reason that Semmelweis was expelled from Vienna. Both challenged conventional medicine and modes of healing. Rochus sought refuge in the forest. He built a hut of boughs and leaves, whereupon a spring arose which supplied water. A dog brought him bread and licked his wounds, healing him. The hunting dog's master, Count Gothard Palastrelli, found Rochus and became his acolyte. Dr. Ignaz Semmelweis sought refuge here, in Buda. Soon he would have acolytes in his hometown, as he'd had in Vienna.

A Conventional Life

"His past no longer spoke to him."—Dr. L.F. Destouches

Semmelweis attempted to lead the semblance of a conventional life—job, home, family—yet was unable to build upon his past accomplishments to any great advantage, that is, his discoveries of an immortal nature.

With the help of affluent friends he'd made during his revolutionary days, he set up a private practice. Throughout revolution, women got pregnant and women gave birth. He delivered women in their homes and at St. Rochus without mishap. Then a "minute and ridiculous" incident occurred, reported by Dr. Destouches, which caused Semmelweis great personal and professional harm. He saved a woman's life and was persecuted for it. Persecution of Semmelweis was a theme Dr. Destouches was reluctant to overlook. He saved a member of the royal family's life and was persecuted for this, too. Here is what happened.

One of his influential friends referred him to a Countess Crandinish. Several other physicians had attended to her and offered different diagnoses, including cancer. One can imagine the royal family's anxiety when the butler let Dr. Semmelweis in and ushers him up to the royal bedroom in order to offer a third opinion.

Semmelweis enters the Countess's chamber. She is receptive. He examines her. Back down at the door, looking grave, he tells the Count in a solemn voice:

"I am sorry. It's cervical cancer, without a doubt."

Night falls, and the royal house is silent.

But then, in the dead of night, comes a pounding at the royal house's door. Gas lamps light, and the butler, struggling with his nightshirt, scurries to the door. Some madman rushes past him then hurtles the stairs—that same Dr. Semmelweis of earlier in the afternoon. He bursts into the bedroom, where the royal couple, countess and count, are fast asleep. Without forewarning, Semmelweis reaches his hand under the covers and makes a gynecological examination. Then, Dr. Semmelweis—

"I was mistaken!" he exclaims, triumphantly. "It's not cancer. Rather, it's a benign tumor."

The royal house overjoyed? A chance good choice of physicians in Semmelweis? An unexpected new lease on life for the countess? Healthy heirs? And, after all, she had submitted to the doctor's examination earlier in the day.

But the doctor's behavior was deemed impulsive, unsettling. And this characterization traveled. Patient after patient left him. His private practice and financial resources dwindled practically to nothing.

Semmelweis lived in a single room up a narrow, winding staircase in an alley off today's fashionable *Lindergasse*. He sold piece by piece of furniture—inherited from his parents?--in order to have his one meal. It would have had to be a small piece, to carry down a winding staircase then transport in his arms to the bazaar.

Then he fell and broke his arm. Go to a doctor? Manufacture his own sling? Soon afterwards, he fell again, this time breaking his leg. He could not feed himself and there was no heat. He was injured, freezing and starving.

Could his siblings not help him? Sister Julianna had married her chemist who inherited his father's chemistry shop, and brother József now owned and operated a large grocery store across from the University of Pest.

News of Semmelweis's condition reaches his friend Lajos in Vienna. Using Dr. Skoda's influence to gain permission to travel, he goes to Budapest. Once there, Lajos is given an address at St. Rochus's hospital and sets out, up and down the narrow alleys off *Lindergasse*. Late at night, he climbs a winding, narrow stairwell...pushes open the door. The room is in shadows. A shadow of a man is in semi-darkness. Lajos approaches, slowly.

"Ignác?"

Later on, by candlelight, Lajos writes to Joseph Skoda.

"At last! I found our friend alive but he has aged so much that I hardly would have recognized him had not his voice led me better than his appearance in the shadows of his room. His features are marked with deep melancholy--for good, I fear. He spoke of you and of Professor Rokitansky in the most affectionate terms. He asked a hundred questions about your life and your health. He said nothing about his material worries, which were all too evident, alas! Armed with your letters of recommendation, I called on Professor Birly [Professor Edi Birly, Director of the St. Rochus Maternity Hospital], who assured me that he would consider Semmelweis for the first vacancy as assistant in his clinic. That would be some sort of justice."

Lajos stayed a few days, then returned to Vienna. He reported to Drs. Skoda, Rokitansky, Hebra, "I found him bedridden and starving."

One morning soon afterwards, another visitor came to Semmelweis's door. He pushed it open.

The door to Semmelweis and his accomplishments is always open.

The visitor says, "Are you Dr. Semmelweis, former Assistant to Professor Klein in Vienna?"

A pair of eyes stares out of the darkness.

It was Professor Gustav Adolf Michaelis's assistant. He'd gone to Vienna as a result of Dr. Hebra's editorial about Semmelweis's findings, which Dr. Michaelis then corroborated.

"If you are he," continues the assistant, "I have a message for you, a painful one but one which favors the cause you espouse." The young man goes on to relate the following:

Dr. Michaelis had instituted chlorine hand washings in his clinic at Kiel and, without washing his own hands, performed the delivery of a beloved niece. She died of puerperal fever a few days later. The next month, Michaelis saw that the mortality rate dropped precipitously in his clinic as a result of the hand washings and realized that his own negligence had killed his niece...slips off to the railway station, waits for the approach of a train, then throws himself in front. The assistant's words:

"So overwhelming was Michaelis' grief, so frightful his despair, that he made an immediate and very detailed investigation into his own responsibility. He could not refute the conclusion that he himself was entirely responsible because, a few days before, he had been treating a number of women stricken with puerperal fever without taking any of the precautions you had indicated and with which he had been long familiar. The obsession which overwhelmed him became one day so piercing, so unbearable, that he threw himself in front of a train."

New Life

"At this moment, Semmelweis emerged from his torpor as though roused by the stinging of this arrow which had just cut through his silence..."—Dr. L.F. Destouches

News of the believing Dr. Michaelis's suicide instilled new life into Semmelweis.

It was essentially from tragedy—such tragic turns of supportive colleagues Kolletschka and Michaelis, and death after death of new mothers and many of their babies from puerperal fever—that Semmelweis drew his courage to continue on. He cleans himself up, dresses then pays a visit to Dr. Birly at St. Rochus's maternity hospital.

Birly, dressed like one in the audience in London and Vienna. In black, bearded, long face...

He wishes to resume his work in obstetrics, Semmelweis informs the good Director.

With Dr. Skoda's letter in hand, and after declaring his admiration for him, Birly says:

"…I am not able in the present state of our Maternity Hospital to offer you work except during the vacation months of July and August. In addition, I must ask you to say nothing to my medical students about this washing their hands in a solution of chloride. That would do us the greatest damage…."

Was Johann Klein's influence so widespread that any maternity hospital that prescribed Semmelweis's procedures lost their official status?

Dr. Birly's views on the origin of childbed fever, Semmeweis knew, included the following: "Uncleanliness of the bowel. The high mortality rate in Vienna was due to their negligence in the administration of purgatives."

First, Klein in Vienna, then Scanzoni in Würtsburg, now Birly in Pest.

As a departure, Semmelweis kept silent and accepted Dr. Birly's terms.

His new job was more than a summer fill-in, for it was during the vacation months that the obstetrical clinic was closed and the hospital admitted maternity patients. He would be plenty busy. He would be at the receiving end of couples who made love and conceived during the hibernating winter season.

For some reason, perhaps riding a ripple of good fortune, in the dead of night, he decides to write his much-delayed book. He may have needed to be away from Vienna and the urgings of his great colleagues to write and publish, which had pushed him over the edge of fear's precipitous cliff into inaction. But now he was encouraged by the positive reception of his lectures and their publication in the medical review *Orvosi Tár*. Most likely there are others reasons, known solely to Semmelweis. At his table, he picks up quill, dips it and begins. Here is the first line:

"Medicine's highest duty is saving threatened human life, and obstetrics is the branch of medicine in which this duty is most obviously fulfilled."

A Spouse

Dr. Destouches, who married his medical school director's daughter and had a daughter with her and would not write a word about his personal life in his great novels, did not write a word about Semmelweis's personal life in his monograph, except to say that romance was a waste of time which Semmelweis did not have. Perhaps for Dr. Destouches, such a quest was redundant because, for him, Semmelweis was already married and he had children. He was married to the hundreds upon hundreds of deceased new mothers he hovered over in the dissection room, scalpel in bloody hand. He was married to the new mothers his means of prevention of childbed fever had saved from such a terrible fate. He was father to the babies who died of the same infection as their mothers. He was father to those babies who survived with a chance at life. Then for Semmelweis, ever unpredictable, life took a momentary kind turn.

He was now thirty-eight years of age, bald, stocky, and his character at this time has been described as "intense," "brusque," "tactless," "gruff," "lacks small talk and pleasantries." Traits hardly enticing for a romance. Nevertheless, he met and fell in love with a young, beautiful Hungarian woman. And she, him. Her name was Maria Wiedenhoffer and she was the daughter of a prosperous Buda-Swabian merchant, just like her father-in-law. She and Ignác shared the same culture, language, spices. The courtship lasted a year and then, in June 1857, they married.

Ignaz and Maria set up a household in the heart of town, in a building on *Váci utca,* a bustling shopping hub and a short-walk to St. Rocha's. The building had a serene central courtyard from which a spiral marble staircase led up to their third-floor flat. Semmelweis spent many a happy morning and evening descending and ascending that staircase, leaving Maria temporarily, only to return to her in the evening.

He was earning a living, however meager. In 1855, he earned 400 florins, equivalent today to several thousand dollars. He was married, had a job and a house. And his youthful wife was pregnant. How odd it must have been for Semmelweis to deliver his own children of a wife and mother so much of a youthful age and outlook of hope and wonderment as the young women who had come to Klein's lying-in clinic in Vienna when he was Clerk of Records. Now, with Maria, he shared some of the same feelings as all those expectant mothers, some of whom made it through, some not.

A newborn cries. Then two, three…five!

He employs all of his experience and skill to deliver his own children in a safe and healthy manner, disinfecting his hands with a solution of chlorine, at home.

He shares his wife's joy. He watches and admires his wife care for their children. Two would die in infancy, not of childbed fever, widening the horizon of grief that Semmelweis experienced in his life and work. New also for him was witnessing the grief of a woman he loved, wife and mother of his children. Semmelweis's horizon of grief over newborns' deaths was deepened by the death of his own.

When commentators write of the drastic physical change that Semmelweis undergoes very soon, from a robust middle-age man to an old one with a sagged body, could it have been over the enormous weight of grief, disappointment and neglect of his work that he had carried for so long? The unsustainable weight of grief over his knowledge that a good many of those young mothers' deaths could have been prevented?

Professor Semmelweis

In 1854, Dr. Birly died, and Semmelweis succeeded him as director of St. Rochus Hospital. At the same time, he was named Professor at the University of Pest.

Had Birly, secretly, through third parties, elected Semmelweis his successor? Was no one else eligible as director to deny and counter Semmelweis's theories? Because such a person would have known exactly what happened: Semmelweis lost no time in putting into practice mandatory washings of the hands with chlorine solution by all physicians. Immediately, he published an "Open Letter to all professors of Obstetrics." It reads:

"Would that my discovery was found to be part of the realm of physics, for one may explain light just as one likes, but that does not prevent it from shining, it is independent of physics. My discovery, alas, depends on obstetricians. That changes everything…"

He sought to improve conditions of St. Rocha's obstetrics unit. It held twenty-nine beds, only three of which were allocated to hard labor, and this room had one window which looked out to a cemetery. There was no enclosed room in which to lecture. Semmelweis had to lecture in the corridors to, at one time, a combined class of squeezed twenty-seven medical students and ninety-three midwives.

No prophet is accepted in his own country.— Jesus Christ

Semmelweis garnered to his immortal work more opposition and outright hatred in his home country than in Vienna. Staff and faculty refused to wash their hands and clean their nails before examinations and deliveries. He had to stand watch. The hospital administration ignored memorandum after memorandum for requests for supplies and instruments. Laundry complained that the obstetrics unit changed bed linen more often than regulations required. Semmelweis purchased supplies of linens with his own money, which went un-reimbursed.

"A kurva anyad!" Semmelweis hurled imprecations at them. It did not improve his stature in their defeated eyes.

Statistics for the academic year 1855-56 were: of 514 women delivered, 2 died of puerperal fever, a mortality rate of 0.39 percent. A resounding success.

Semmelweis was forever attempting to clarify his positions. If he were alive today, he would, most likely, do the same: examine, correct, amplify. His work is unfinished. His work continues.

Semmelweis's biographer William Sinclair (1909)* provides a lively picture of Semmelweis in the act of doing something which he truly hated, write, and his state of mind:

"He worked feverishly through 1858, '59, '60, continually writing fresh chapters, all in a great hurry, constantly repeating portions without coordination, and hurrying the ms. off to the printers without revision."

His book received very poor reviews. Dr. Nuland summarizes:

"...inserting paragraphs and entire sections inappropriately...compulsive need to add new chapters even when he had already covered the same ground...he seems never to have reviewed the text as it was taking shape...sometimes confused..."

His book does not proceed in chronological order. He could be discussing the commission of

1846 in which the foreign students* caused the Scourge by their rough handling of women in term and then, without segue, to having already found the causes and means of prevention of childbed fever. Semmelweis's own translator F. P. Murphy:

"The style is wordy and repetitious. The argument flows back and forth without progressing to any logical point; the author is egotistic and bellicose. We are conscious of S's mental aberration and feeling of persecution...the books itself discloses the underlying paranoia."

Time is always the present. Past, present and future are one and the same. Semmelweis's life and career is always present. At any one given time, thousands—350 thousand to be exact--of women are in the act of childbirth.

Would have it been better if he had not undertaken this writing? Attempt to satisfy its need of ten years before soon after his discoveries? So that now, his hatred of anything to do with the act of writing and publishing a lot of it opened the way for his digressers to pursue him, say it's outdated, with little scientific proof now as it was then, just when he was attempting to make a new life.

And then one year after his book was published, Semmelweis added to his grief by publishing *Open Letters to Sundry Professors of Obstetrics*. It is comprised of curses, denouncements, the afterlife. He addressed Scanzoni directly:

"I denounce you before God as murderer!"

Semmelweis expounded:

"Scanzoni has so often shown himself to be a wretched observer that I cannot accept his observations regarding the connection between, for example, emotional disturbance and puerperal fever. I am much more of the opinion that in his many observed cases, either he or someone else infected the patient and that between the time of the infection and the outbreak of fever, emotional disturbances occurred."

Professor Créde, Director of Obstetrics and Gynecology at the Charité in Berlin, and Professor of Obstetrics in Leipzig, wrote:

"Semmelweis calls everyone who disagrees with him an ignoramus and a murderer."

Scanzoni had gone so far as to compose and circulate a petition* to the Bohemian Provincial Government that it was he who shed light on the nature and origin of "this malicious disease." Semmelweis responded:

"The petition proves the truth of my claim that Scanzoni is more concerned about who gets credit, *rechthalberei,* than about discovering the truth."

Semmelweis indicted his successor as Assistant in the First Clinic, Carl Braun, in a slightly different manner:

"He should take some semesters in Logic."

Finally, Semmelweis had made himself intolerable. He wanted the mere mention of his name to be venomous. His failure to provide documented clinical evidence had caused him to become bitter, which, in turn, moved him toward madness and a brutal death. How facile he had made it to dismiss his prescriptions against puerperal fever now. Klein and his faction were right. Semmelweis was quite mad.

Feedback, Again

The career of Ignaz Semmelweis was never lacking in efforts to spread the word about his discoveries. It was never lacking in feedback that tormented him. It was said that, temperamentally, he was unable to cope with adversity and criticism.

He continued to work while he coped with the unnecessary deaths of new mothers.

Once again, Semmelweis and colleagues conferred, collaborated in writing and stuffing envelopes and mailing. His assistant Dr. Jozsef Fleischer sent a report of that excellent low mortality rate of 0.39 due to Dr. Semmelweis's *Lehr* to the journal *Wiener medizinische Wochenschrift*.

Again, they waited for feedback. Semmelweis devoted the last 200 pages of his 500-page book to, and much of the last reservoir of his energy, to— "Reactions to My Teachings: Correspondence and Published Opinions."

At this time, one of Ignaz and Maria's infants died, and they grieved.

Some outreach efforts reaped silence. Some returned which disappointed. For the most part, he and his *Lehr* were old news, the consensus feedback indicated. Fleischer's report was printed with an editorial note, which read:

"We thought that this theory of chlorine disinfection had died out long ago; the experience and the statistical evidence of most of the lying-in institutions protest against the opinions expressed in this article: it would be well that our readers should not allow themselves to be misled by this theory at this present time."

Sound like Dr. Johann Klein? Not exactly, as Klein had recently passed away into medical history infamy, but the appenda was written by Klein's successor, Dr. Carl Braun. Semmelweis responded:

"In 1854 in Vienna, the birthplace of my theory, 400 maternity patients died from childbed fever. In published medical works, my teachings are either ignored or attacked.

"Even now (1859) back in Vienna, physicians officially functioning in the First and Second Clinics still are opposed to my opinion regarding the origin of childbed fever."

How many women had died unnecessarily in Vienna, at the hands of Klein and now Braun?

Semmelweis wrote, despairingly:

"Of all the obstetricians I know, that poor Michaelis is decidedly the first and only one of whom it might be said that he had too great a professional conscience."

Poor Michaelis. He had overlooked disinfecting his hands and inadvertently infected his niece and orphaned her child.

Yes, Semmelweis was bitter. He had regrets. Pursuit by old enemies nailed him to the present. He wrote:

"The years 1849-'50 may have been even more favorable had my request to direct the First Clinic been granted."

In general, he made little distinction whether the reactions to his teachings occurred in 1847-50 or now, ten years later, after his book was published. Time conflated. As far as the medical community was concerned, women died just as well at any moment, in all years, in all maternity facilities around the world. Opposition was forever. Opposition killed women in childbirth.

Had his work reached American shores? In the United States during the 1920s, half of maternal deaths were caused by puerperal fever. For a disease, Semmelweis wrote, that was "preventable by ordinary intelligence and careful training."

Childbed fever was not endemic in the United States for the reason that students and physicians did not go from Dissection to the maternity clinics.

Semmelweis's conflation of time that must have pleased Kurt Vonnegut one century later carried toward the very end of his, Semmelweis's, mortal life, to the last hours of his rational mind. It ends with thoughts of the professor who succeeded him as Assistant in the First Clinic in Vienna, Carl Braun. After presenting pages of Braun's "inappropriate circumstances that can cause childbed fever," Semmelweis concludes:

"The reader will note with astonishment that Carl Braun, the same Carl Braun who totally rejects the speculative hypothesis of cadaverous infection, who to the satisfaction of every true friend of humanity has successfully restored the unrestricted operation of epidemic influences. Oh Logic! In taking leave of our Viennese colleague, we recommend most urgently that if he should again feel called upon to fight for the epidemic deaths of maternity patients, he should first attend at least one semester of logic."

The death toll of new mothers climbed. Semmelweis observed that the alarming number of deaths was restricted to mothers but not their newborns. New mothers had contracted the Fever post-partum, during recovery. Laundry, the cause was dirty linen. Semmelweis announced. To save money, administration had contracted laundry to an inferior launderer. Semmelweis goes into the delivery and recovery wards and brings those bed sheets up to his nose: that foul odor of decomposed discharges. Semmelweis complained, forcefully. Nothing was done. Semmeweis takes it upon himself to wash and dry bedclothes. He gathers bundles of used linens in his arms and then marches into the administrator's office, one von Tandler, and dumps the stinking heap on his desk. The laundry contractor is changed. Semmelweis earned two new enemies: administrator von Tandler and the head nurse in charge of linens.

Wilhelm Scanzoni returns to hound him. Semmelweis writes toward the end of his sanity:

"...Scanzoni says Lumpe and Zipfl have agreed with him. The facts are these. On 15 May 1850, at the general meeting of the Imperial Society of Physicians in Vienna, I delivered a lecture on the origin and prevention of childbed fever. A discussion followed...in it, Lumpe and Zipfl spoke against me. But Chiari, Arneth, Helm and [Anton] Hayne supported my position..."

This was the lecture Semmelweis chose not to publish and Minutes were taken and his adversaries published their full comments. These were remembered and disseminated.

Dr. Arneth

A young, active, generous advocate took up in Budapest where Drs. Skoda, Routh, Rokitansky, Hebra and Haller had left off in Vienna.

Dr. Franz Hector Arneth was willing to travel to Paris for the purpose of presenting and defending Semmelweis's prescriptions to the Medical Society of Paris, which was holding a conference on the subject of childbed fever from 23 February to 6 July 1858. Arneth and Semmelweis projected in their fiery imaginations the great scientists of Paris performing official experiments and then, only a short time later, confirming the results and publishing them. The two collected funds for the journey and several weeks' stay in Paris. Arneth could not attend the entire conference, which would continue on through the spring into the summer. He could stay a week or so. A passport was difficult to obtain. The various European states were foreign countries in relation one to the other.

Once again in the life of Ignaz Semmelweis, a major event unfolded at the onset of spring. With the precious manuscript clutched to his chest, Dr. Routh set out in a stagecoach for Paris, a journey of eight days. Writes Dr. Destouches:

"No sign revealed to those who met him on the way to Paris that this poor, lonely traveler, the son of a second-rate nation, carried in his luggage a sheaf of papers more precious than all the secret books of all the Indies, that he was the bearer of a wonderful truth, the simple reading of which might every year save the lives of thousands of human beings, and spare them infinite suffering…if he were to speak of what he knew, he would bore everyone; if he insisted too much, might he have been killed?"

Arneth attends each and every meeting, attentive, at the edge of his seat. A look of horror comes over his face once he understands that the assemblage of notable obstetricians do not want to know the truth. What did this bright young man feel when, following references to Semmelweis's *Lehr,* the most celebrated obstetrician of his time, Dr. Dubois, summed up the opinions of those gathered:

"This theory of Semmelweis which…provoked such violent polemics in obstetrical circles, no less in Austria than in other countries, seems today to be completely abandoned, even in the school in which it was first professed.

"It may be that it did contain a few good principles but its scrupulous application presented such difficulties that it was necessary, in Paris, for instance, to place the hospital staff in quarantine for a large part of the year, and that, moreover, for an altogether problematical result."

But young Arneth did not lose faith or courage. He applied for permission that experiments be undertaken in maternity hospitals modeled after those Semmelweis had performed in Vienna. Doors slammed in Arneth's face. Dubois of Paris became the Klein of Vienna. His influence spread like a cancer of Denial. Arneth toured the great maternity clinics in Paris. He reported to Semmelweis:

"The Maternité clinic is used exclusively for the education of midwives, yet the mortality rate is as great as Dubois' Paris clinic for the education of physicians. It's regrettable that the autopsy room is so near to Delivery. Midwives contaminate their hands with decaying matter."

Arneth sent a report by Dr. Johann Friedrich Osiander*, who described Paris' Maternité as follows:

"Autopsies were conducted in a building in the garden somewhat removed from the maternity hospital; these were usually attended by student midwives. I was often astonished to see the active part some of the young women took in the dissection of the corpses. With bare and bloody hands, holding large knives in their hands, laughing and quarreling, they cut the pelvis apart, having received permission from the physician to prepare the corpse for him."

Arneth returned to Budapest, discouraged. He tried to convince Semmelweis of the truth of all that he had seen and heard.

Semmelweis would not hear of it. The weight of years of comprehensive denial, of countless, unnecessary loss of life fell upon his shoulders. He made little distinction whether the negative reactions to his teachings occurred in 1847 or in 1860. He continued to conflate time. Women died as well at any moment, in all years, in all maternity wards around the world. Opposition was forever.

"Arneth remained reasonable. Semmelweis could be no longer... He had lost his lucidity, that power of all powers, that concentration of all our hopes upon one specific point in the Universe."— Dr. Destouches.

He had gone mad.

PART V: The Madness and Death of Ignaz P. Semmelweis

"Madness turned the wheel of its torture."—Dr. L.F. Destouches

Ailing Semmelweis, graphite pencil, Aharon Gluska,
2019

If the decline of his mental health appears
sudden, in this and other narratives, one reason is
that only his wife, Maria Wiedenhoffer, noted its
onset, tracked its evolution, transported him to the
asylum in Vienna and attempted to visit with him
just before he was killed.

Instances of Chance like that of life in the
street when he was a boy, encountering the guitarist

of loose strings, later on skipping law class and attending a demonstration by Dr. Joseph Skoda, taking a trip to Venice and finding pleasure, the chance that the untimely death of Jakob Kolletschka would lead him to the truth about childbed fever— now, the surprise of things, the unknown, the wonder and his destiny to end his days as an conscious important scientist, loving husband and father, were largely out of his hands.

Her husband began to show signs of insanity in 1861, his wife said, around the time he finished his book, four years before. Was she aware of his fear, his trepidation of everything to do with writing? Unknown, underlying obstacles, physical, chemical…. Still he'd gone ahead at a time when life seemed to promise a bit more, love, home, children, and writes his book and then, like all of us, waits…vulnerable, naked. He weathers the overall trashing, a kind of intellectual, emotional and work-wise murder, of his self, his person, his work and any hope he may have had that the stakes, a new mother's life and that of her child, would win out over stupidity, envy. "Writing" and all its incipient terrors have a way of brimming over. His wife may have been aware of at least some of them. Maria points to a particular event.*

During the summer of 1865, on July 21, edelweiss in bloom in Budapest and in Vienna, Semmelweis is slated to present a report in regards to filling a vacant appointment on his university faculty. Sweating, bent over, dressed slovenly, aged beyond recognition, he walks to the lectern, withdraws a piece of paper from his pocket and looks down. It's the text of the midwife's oath.*

"Do…no…harm…Don't…do…anything…you… cannot… fix…."

Members of the audience turn and stare into one another's eyes, mouths agape. A few colleagues, regardless of their views about childbed fever, approach and gently lead the poor doctor away.

Semmelweis, expressionless…. His spirit has left his body, the way the spirits of so many new mothers and newborns had left *their* bodies.

A few days later, Maria calls in Dr. Janos Bokai, a friend and pediatrician. A pediatrician to assess the mental health of an obstetrician. Semmelweis is also bewildered. Unless Bokai has come to tend to one of the children. But no, he questions him, then reports to his wife, according to Dr. Destouches, "He's mentally ill, physically strong." Bokai adds much of what Maria already knows. Ignaz has been drinking heavily and engaged in heightened sexual activity. Does his wife corroborate? Which does not in themselves amount to mental illness. Dr. Bokai continues:

"…intercourse with prostitutes after years of faithfulness to his wife, frequent masturbation, indecency toward acquaintances and strangers. Grandiose ideas such as having 100 photos taken of himself to be sent along with copies of his book."

Authors often accompany their published books with all sorts of promotional material, including autographed photos. An old wives' remedy for frequent masturbation is a walk through a cemetery. Dr. Semmelweis was certainly well acquainted with the cemeteries of Vienna and Budapest. All he had to do was look out his hospital windows.

Other educated guesses in regard to his precipitous mental and physical decline.

"Persecution"—Dr. Destouches.

" Perhaps Alzheimer's disease"--Dr. Nuland.*

"Perhaps Syphilis" –Dr. Jones. Plausible, given his frequenting of prostitutes at an early age, in Buda then in Vienna, now in Budapest. Late stage-syphilis is known to damage the brain.

Recently, Dr. Bokai reports, Semmelweis had taken a lover who is a prostitute.

Consorting with a favorite prostitute, perhaps, was a fleeting moment of sheer pleasure, outside the pale of viewing a woman as pregnant or as an agent of propagating the race, a momentary reprieve from saving her from infection. All those diseased new mothers he looked down upon in the Dead Room and Dissection flash before his eyes. Now, in their places, lying with a woman paid, this woman of the night, her health not of immediate concern.

"Now he wandered with the mad, into the absolute, into those glacial solitudes where our passions no longer awaken echoes...."—Dr. L.F. Destouches

His manner of dress changes from meticulousness to slovenliness.

His speech betrays him.

"The words he uttered did not convey what he intended and were most often meaningless," writes Dr. Nuland.

He's discovered digging into a wall. Semmeweis turns to whoever stormed in on him.

"I'm searching," he says, "for great secrets buried there by a priest friend of mine."

Major personages of his past penetrate the shifting maze of his dementia.

There's Gustav Michaelis—no! no!—comes a roaring train. Joseph Skoda—hulking, ear to a chest, now listening, now spouting coarse innuendoes. Johann Klein—"livid with all the hatred of an infernal world"—pointing at him. Newborns with the Scourge cry...cry! Semmelweis breaks out into a run, chasing his phantoms down the staircase, into the street... weighed down by cruelty, stupidity. Cheeks dropped to jowls. His eyes recede into shadow. He begins to move in an "eccentric fashion."

Unattached Professor

This disoriented, hallucinatory phase of the madness of Ignaz Semmelweis continues until the spring of 1865. He manages to lecture, on gynecology. That way he can keep a step ahead of the hounds. Even then, however, his mind was ever occupied by his favorite subject. He projects back to his Assistantship in Vienna, greeting and admitting smiling, young, pregnant women...exchanging the personnel of Clinics I & II...in Venice gazing up in awe at an original Titian...colleague Kolletschka's finger pricked accidentally and then suffering and dying in the same manner as a new mother... a wave of new mothers breathe their last...their very last....

Someone, maybe his wife, takes him by the arm to his university.

Often, when speaking to his class, his excitement rose to such a degree as to cause alarm to those around him. His students stare. His wife takes his arm again and leads him away.

Suddenly, a calm descends. It's his final spring, though it's warm like all the others, air redolent with flowers. He's allowed to take walks by himself. He does not wear a hat. Going hatless out on the street tantamount to a shaved head inside an asylum. Everyone knows him…slow motion passersby, nodding, tipping *their* hats. Step aside for the once-famous, now-crazy doctor. He seems not to recognize a soul. But was his madness total?

Late at night, in the privacy of his room, he takes up charcoal and paper and creates a manifesto. He writes quickly in large black letters, in perfect Hungarian:

"Fathers of families! Do you know what it means to call to the bedside of your wife in labor a doctor or a midwife? It means you are voluntarily forcing her to run the risk of losing her life, so easily avoided by these measures…"

He copies his manifesto a handful of times and then, clutching his sheets, steals into the street— not a soul in view—and hurriedly pastes them up on one wall, then another.…

On his way home, suddenly, he bursts out running… looking back over his shoulder. He darts into the anatomy theater, which he still recognizes. A dissection lesson is underway, corpse in the center surrounded by instructor and students.

"Make way!" and Semmelweis pushes through, knocking over chairs…picks up a scalpel. Everyone knows who he is, enough of his specter remains, but no one can look him in the eye. Before he can be restrained from cutting deep into the putrid tissues, he slices off shreds of muscle and then tosses them hither and yon. Blood splattering, tissue flying. He's mumbling, seeking to explain. At this point, no one is even trying to understand him. Then, with the scalpel blade and his fingers, he rummages around in a cavity reeking with liquefaction. Dr. Destouches continues with this phase of Semmelweis's madness:

"With a movement more convulsive than before, he cut himself deeply. His wound bled. He cried out. He made threats. He was disarmed. A crowd gathered around him. But it was too late… As Kolletschka not long since, he had just infected himself fatally."

His colleagues at the university grasp the opportunity to replace him. Semmelweis is not indispensable. But let him retain the title, "Unattached Professor." Some semblance of recognition. It's with his last professional title, "Unattached Professor," that Ignaz P. Semmelweis marches into History. A "free" Semmelweis, timeless, physician to all.

Last Days

Drs. Destouches and Nuland provide different narratives of his last days. They are in agreement that he was taken from Budapest to Vienna, where he was placed in a public asylum, beaten there, and died.

According to Dr. Nuland*:

His wife, Maria Weidenhoffer, is persuaded to admit her husband to the public insane asylum in Vienna. Her husband's behavior described above moves her to this decision. Semmelweis's friend János Balassa, professor of surgery, signs the document that commits him.

A pediatrician and a surgeon diagnosis and act on his dementia.

Then Maria makes secret arrangements through the telegraph with Dr. Ferdinand Hebra in Vienna. Remember Hebra, first among colleagues? Another of Joseph Skoda's protégées... they'd sat side by side and wrote letters to which they attached their hearts. Maria persuades Hebra and tells her husband that they are going to Vienna in order to visit his, Professor Hebra's, new sanatorium. His great old colleague has done so well for himself.

They take the new overnight train from Budapest to Vienna. Maria carries their baby girl, Antonia. Her uncle accompanies them. Semmelweis does not know where he is nor where he is going. The ride is long, he does not know. His past and his future flee past his window.

Dr. Hebra awaits at the Vienna station. He is older, his look, sullen. He mentions the new private sanatorium recently opened. Semmelweis listens, blankly. Maria hands Hebra the Detaining Order signed by three doctors, none of whom were psychiatrists. Then Hebra escorts Semmelweis to "New Institutes," a Viennese insane asylum located in *Lazarettgasse (Landes-Irren-Anstalt in der Lazarettgasse)*, known for its common, rough 700 inmates.

Semmelweis finds himself in the asylum's lush gardens...looks up, around. At first, he trusts what appear to be familiar faces and voices. Three representatives, not doctors, form a circle around him in the front garden. It is late July. Edelweiss in full bloom. Semmelweis speaks animatedly with a staff member who is accustomed to new arrivals.

Suddenly, a cognitive flash. He surmises what's happening...attempts to flee. Dr. Hebra and Maria, Antonia in her arms, and her uncle back away. He's caught, severely beaten by several guards--big psyche aides--secured in a straitjacket, dragged inside and confined to a darkened cell. Apart from the straitjacket, treatments at this asylum include dowsing with cold water and doses of castor oil.

According to Dr. Destouches--

It's an older, worn, illustrious Dr. Joseph Skoda in Vienna, first among his teachers and mentors, who hears Semmelweis's urgent call. From

Lajos, perhaps, or Hebra or Maria. He sets out for Budapest, his mission to fetch his ill protégée and accompany him to a mental hospital back in Vienna.

Somehow Skoda manages to pack him into the train for the long journey back to Vienna. Side by side with him, train flying....How painful for Skoda, all his wits about him, aware of the historical figure sitting beside him, forlornly, one foot in eternity.

Skoda sits, dejected, in his train compartment. Recalls that first day when this law student named Semmelweis audited his demonstration of a fever victim in the hospital basement...edges into the circle around himself, watching, listening. There was no way of knowing his potential then. Semmelweis had realized that himself, to his great peril. They arrive in Vienna on 22 June 1865, the height of spring, Semmelweis's last.

Once in Vienna, Dr. Destouches continues, Skoda knows exactly where he has to take his ward.

He'd worked in Vienna's public asylum early in his career, in 1826. When Semmelweis was eight years old and just about to venture out into the wider world, Joseph Skoda was already amid the certified insane in this very place, assistant to that same infamous Johann Klein. Klein had banished Skoda to the public asylum on the pretext that he "tired out patients by sounding them too frequently." Those crazy doctors. One with palpitations and auscultations. The other with the washings of hands.

Skoda takes Semmelweis's arm and leads him inside. He releases him to several attendants. Skoda skulks behind. He hears the broken man's short, halting steps…his frightened breaths about to lose their miracle.

All accounts agree that the day after her husband's confinement, Maria Weidenhoffer comes to visit her husband and is greeted by the asylum director, Mr. Hofrath Riedel. Her husband, he tells her, had tried to escape and had to be forcibly restrained by six attendants. She was not allowed to see him.

Two weeks later, on August 14, 1865, Ignaz Philipp Semmelweis died.

"His discovery exceeded the power of his genius. That, perhaps, was the deepest cause of all of his misfortunes."--Dr. L.F. Destouches

Any attempt on this writer's part to describe the last hours, the way this great man was treated, cannot adequately approach their horror. It's best that another writer much greater than I attempt same. Dr. Destouches, for example. His talent as a novelist, which Kurt Vonnegut so admired, appeared early, in *his* description of some of those same hours, Semmelweis's last:

"Twenty times night fell in that room before death carried away the one who had issued it so specific and unforgettable a challenge. In the end, it claimed only the shadow of a man, a delirious, corrupted form, whose contours were being worn away by a creeping pestilence…. The progress of the infection had been so slow, so systematic he was not spared a single battle along the road to rest. Lymphangitis… peritonitis…pleurisy….When the turn came for meningitis, he began to babble a sort of endless verbal stream. On the morning of 16 August, Death seized him by the throat. He suffocated. Putrid odors flooded the room. But he clung on in this world as long as one can with an impossible brain and a body in tatters. He seemed to have fainted, lost in shadow, when one last revolt, very near the end, brought him up toward the light and the pain.

"Suddenly, he raised himself up on his bed. They had to force him down again. 'No! No!' he cried out. It seems that in the depths of this being there could be no indulgence for the common fate, for Death, and nothing was possible for him but an enormous faith in life. He was heard again to call, 'Skoda! Skoda!' Dr. Skoda had stayed with him to the very end. Semmelweis entered into peace at seven o'clock that evening."

"He was definitely bludgeoned to death."

Writes Dr. Irvine Loudon*:

"Newly discovered papers suggest septicaemia, probably staphylococcal, because the notes taken in the asylum describe an illness with multiple septic skin lesions like boils or carbuncles and the ravings of a man in a fever.

"Those papers first entry: he was tricked.

"Second day: confined to a straitjacket.

"Six days later: in a frenzied moment was terribly excited—he knew he was going to die—he hit, shoved, tongue very dry…breathed with difficulty…middle finger very gangrenous…boils everywhere. Blue color, rambling speech….

"Last day's entry includes: 'intensive collapsus' and 'pyaemia'.

"On July 31, one entry: 'recognizes the doctor'. Arrived with severe infection of the middle finger that turned gangrenous and septicemia may have been the cause of death. Suggested that the real cause of death was forcible restraint by the asylum attendants: he was definitely bludgeoned to death."

The Autopsy of Dr. Ignaz Semmelweis

His body was transferred to the Pathological Institute of *Allgemeine Krankenhaus*, the site of his great discoveries. The very place where young Doctor Semmelweis looked down into the faces of hundreds of hopeful new mothers and newborns and heard their cries. His material remains are placed on a table in the dissection room. He takes the place of all those women and babies. The following description comes from the official autopsy protocol, obtained by the Hungarian physician Dr. Georg Silló-Seidl from Viennese archives in 1977.

"It is with sadness that Gustav Scheuthauer, Professor Rokitansky's assistant, performs the autopsy.

"The appearance of the body shows injuries to the left hand, four fingers of the right hand, both arms and the chest—all of which support his wife's account of events. Her husband was beaten by asylum personnel within the hour of his admittance. Injury to the left chest indicates that he was stomped upon as he lay on the floor. This injury consists of a discolored green skin abscess under which protrudes a 'half-sphere swelling like an air-pillow,' which, on cutting open the body, was found to be caused by an extensive collection of 'yellow-green pus…mixed with stinking gases' located between the chest muscles and the rib cage.

"He was definitely beaten."

In death, Semmelweis produces that stench that had become so familiar to him.

Burial

Dr. Ignaz Philipp Semmelweis was buried in Vienna on August 15, 1865. Brief announcements of his death appeared in a few medical periodicals in Vienna and Budapest. Although the rules of the Hungarian Association of Physicians and Natural Scientists specified that a commemorative address be delivered in honor of a member who had died in the preceding year, there was no such address for Semmelweis. His death was never even mentioned. A few people attended the service. His wife, Maria Weidenhoffer, did not.

Dr. János Diescher was appointed Semmelweis's successor at the Pest University maternity clinic. Immediately, mortality rates jumped six fold to 6%.

Interment

Dr. Ignaz Semmelweis's remains were transferred to Budapest in 1891. On 11 October 1964, they were transferred to the house in Tában in which he was born, in the shadows of St. Stephen's church. The house is now a museum and a library. Every spring edelweiss bloom.

Edelweiss, Edelweiss, every morning you
greet me,small and white, clean and bright, you look
happy to meet me.Blossom of snow, may you bloom
and grow, bloom and grow forever.
Edelweiss, Edelweiss, bless my homeland forever.

EPILOGUE

St. Rochus returned incognito to his hometown of Montpellier, where he was arrested as a spy upon the betrayal of an uncle and thrown into prison. He languished in jail five years, still unknown. But he knew who he was and the blessings bestowed upon him. On the day he died, 16 August 1327, the hand of an angel laid a tablet beneath his head inscribed in gold, God granting him, "Who that calleth meekly to St. Rochus shall not be hurt by pestilence."

In his home country of Budapest, Hungary there is a Semmelweis convent, the Semmelweis Medical History Museum and the Semmelweis Klinic, a hospital for women in Vienna.

A reflex is named for him. The Semmelweis Reflex: human behavior characterized by the reflex rejection of new knowledge that goes against entrenched norms, beliefs, paradigms.

A surge of happiness when those countless anonymous mothers learned about Dr. Semmelweis, how he had helped them, and their children....

Chronology of the Life of Ignaz P. Semmelweis (1818-1865)

1818 – born, 18 July, town of Tában, Budapest, Hungary; fourth son of nine children.

1837 – enrolls as student of Law, Vienna University.

1838 – exchanges the study of law for the study of medicine.

1844 –obtains medical degree, Vienna University; promoted to degree of Master of Midwifery.

1845-46—apprenticed for two years under Professor Rokitansky; November: appointed Master of Surgery.

1846 – accepted as doctor of Obstetrics. Begins two-year appointment as Assistant to First Clinic Director Johann Klein, Vienna Imperial Hospital.

1846-47 (winter)--studies English for planned trip to Ireland; March: trip to Venice.

1847--one of the most important years in the history of Obstetrics. One of the most important years in the history of women. Dr. Semmelweis discovers the origins of puerperal fever and its mean of prevention.

1847-1851—Semmelweis refuses to publish his findings. Colleagues write letters and lecture announcing and promoting his work. Responses, now and until the end of his life, are mixed.

1847--run-up year to the Europe-wide revolutions of 1848. A new pope, Pius VI, was elected who, at first, appeared progressive. He granted amnesty to revolutionaries who had exiled themselves from Europe to distant lands during the previous decades. Born and raised in the shadows of the Congress of Vienna, these revolutionaries had come of age, and were returning home. Semmelweis partakes of protest activities in Vienna and Budapest.

1849—assistantship term in Vienna hospital expires; It is not renewed.

1850—applies for position of privat-dozent which is denied. Reapplies and is accepted on the condition that he teach without the use of cadavers; May: delivers lecture on the origin and prevention of childbed fever, Imperial Society of Physicians in Vienna.

1851—leaves Vienna hastily. Assumes unpaid, honorary head physician of St. Rochus's Hospital Obstetrical ward.

1855–named Director of Obstetrics & Professor of Theoretical and Practical Obstetrics, University of Pest.

1856–delivers three lectures on "The Etiology of puerperal fever" published in seven issues of the Medical Weekly. Kapolnai, "An Overview of University Education", 31.

1857—begins writing his long-awaited book; June: marries Maria Wiedenhoffer, daughter of a Buda-Swabian prominent merchant. He is 39. She is 18. They would have five children: a son who died shortly after birth; a daughter who died at four months; a second daughter who lived to adulthood; a second son who committed suicide at twenty-three; the eldest, a daughter, who went on to marry and have children.

1858—January: appointed Privat-dozent, University of Pest; May: appointed unpaid, honorary Director of Obstetrics, St. Rochus hospital, Pest.

1857–resigns as Director of Obstetrics, St. Rochus hospital.

1861-- publishes his masterwork *Die Aetiologie, der Begriffe und die Prophylaxis des Kindbettfiebers* (The Etiology , the Concept, and the Prophylaxis of Childbed Fever)

1865—August: confined to a public insane asylum where, on August 13, he is murdered.

Acknowledgements

Dr. Ignaz Semmelweis for his life and work and inspiration to live and perform mine. Ellen Nerenberg, field manager, for her undying belief, support, and brilliance. Massimiliano Zantedeschi, partner in work. Aharon Gluska and his great pencil sketch of a young Semmelweis for rooting Semmelweis and myself in the living, breathing present. Graphic designer extraordinaire Dave Barry for understanding and capturing the heart and soul of this project through his designs. Professor of anthropology and film studies and author Dr. Akös Östor who generously devoted his time and insights, allowing approach to the heart, culture and history of Semmelweis. Dr. Prakash Sampath, neurosurgeon and President of the Rhode Island Neurological Institute, whose presence in this project about Semmelweis's life and work established in an informed, eloquent way Semmelweis's place and importance in medical history and the myriad ways his contributions continue on to this day. I wrote the heart of it in the home of Lotus Kendra and want to thank her for her beautiful place and soul.

Contributors

Dave Barry: Experienced Art Director & Graphic Designer. Accomplished, well traveled musician/keyboard player with over fifteen album credits. Dave designed the original Hand Sanitizer with female symbol and bloody hand. He says, "I am ever conscious of beauty, budget and deadlines."

Dr. Elizabeth C. Jones: Pediatrician. Graduated one of six women from Tulane Medical School class of 1952. Following internships and residencies in Florida and Hawaii and a fellowship in child psychiatry at Children's Memorial Hospital, Chicago, Illinois, she entered private pediatric practice in Evanston, Illinois (1957-1982).

Ellen V. Nerenberg: Hollis Professor of Romance Languages and Literatures, Wesleyan University. Author of the prize-winning *Prison Terms; Murder Made in Italy. Body of State: The Moro Affair, A Nation Dividea* (Fairleigh-Dickinson U P, 2011).by Marco Baliani, with Professor Nicoletta Marini-Maio.

Aharon Gluska: internationally renowned artist. Gluska received grants from the National

Endowment of the Arts. Pollack-Krasner Foundation. Aharon was one of two winners of the 1996 Zussman Prize for artists dealing with the Holocaust, from the Yad Vashem museum, for his paintings of prisoners at Auschwitz based on photographs of them taken by their Nazi guards. His art is displayed in the Tel Aviv Museum of Art, Jewish Museum, New York City, and the Brooklyn Museum, and many others.

Ákös Őstor: anthropologist, scholar, professor emeritus Wesleyan University. His books include *The Play of the Gods: Locality, Ideology, Structure, and time in the Festivals of a Bengali Town,* and with Professor Lina Fruzzetti of Brown University, *Calcutta Conversations, Concepts of Person,* and co-directed with Professor Fruzzetti films *Serpent Mother, Seed and Earth, Singing Pictures. Fishers of Dar.*

Prakash Sampath M.D.: surgeon. President, Rhode Island Neurological Institute.

Benjamin **Travers**: Writer/Director/Producer. Visual/audio production. Producer/Director of forthcoming documentary Semmelweis, the Women's Doctor.

NOTES

*The history of Puerperal Fever pre-Semmelweis can be found here: https://babel.hathitrust.org/cgi/pt?id=njp.3210106 8770021;view=1up;seq=42

* Dr. Louis Ferdinand Destouches, a.k.a. Louis Ferdinand Céline. Destouches was a student in medical school when he submitted his book *The Life and Work of Semmelweis* as his Thesis in Medicine at Paris, 1924. Céline would become one of the most important novelists of the twentieth century. What was there about Céline's brief life of Semmelweis that intrigued novelist Kurt Vonnegut so? I believe he was intrigued that Céline was a student when he wrote his creative biography and knew, at least instinctually, that his thesis would become as important as Semmelweis' medical thesis *The Life of Plants.* Vonnegut and the rest of us are fortunate to have the perspective of considering in combination Céline's youthful work with his electric talent as a novelist. For Vonnegut, Céline was close enough to his medical training to experience passion for his subject, recognize his, Semmeweis', monumental compassion.

*Walter Benjamin(1892-1940)--German Jewish philosopher, cultural critic and essayist.

*midwives. For a discussion of women in the medical profession, *see The Rise of the Medical Profession* by Noel Parry and Jose Parry (London: Croom Helm, 1976)

*Dr. Sherwin. B. Nuland (1930-2014) – prominent surgeon/author of the seminal book on Semmelweis, titled *The Doctor's Plague.* (W.W. Norton & Co. copyright©2003 Sherwin B. Nuland.

*Joseph Skoda, (1805-1881), Semmelweis's mentor

*Karl von Rokitansky (1804-1878). Master surgeon, teacher and mentor.

*Leopold Aunbrügger (1722-1809). Forerunner of Semmelweis's; Known for his pioneering work on percussion.

*Jean-Nicolas Corvisart (1755-1828). Corvisart's book was published in 1806(with C. E. Horeau; translated into English by Jacob Gates as "An essay on the organic diseases and lesions of the heart and great vessels" (1812).

*Christian Joseph Berres (1796-1844). Pioneer in photomicrography--producing photomicrographs via the daguerreotype.

*Serious physicians knew Rokitansky's multi-volume *Handbuch der pathologischen Anatomie*. The great physician wrote: "First …sorting out the facts scientifically on a purely anatomically basis…second demonstrating the applicability of the facts and their utilization for diagnosis in live patients."

*Dr. Johann Boër. In 1784, Queen Maria Theresa's heir Josef II had founded the finest obstetrics department in Europe. "It must have a cosmopolitan director," Josef II said, so he appointed Dr. Johann Boër and then sent him off straightaway to study in England and France. After a year, Boër returned to Vienna and was named professor of midwifery and director of the lying-in-hospital. If Dr. Boër could have continued as director, and not given way to Klein in 1823, the story of childbed fever around the world and of Ignaz Semmelweis in particular would most likely have been very different. Adopting gentle techniques and natural methods of the British accoucheurs, Boër ordered his staff to limit the number of internal exams during labor and to use instrumental delivery, mainly forceps, as a last resort.

"Whatever is done artificially," Boër had stated, "apart from this given necessity, is mere bungling, serving only to torture and destroy mother and child."

Boër dissected new mothers who had died of the Fever solely to study the pathology that had killed them. He refused to allow instruction on the corpses of dead mothers. This was a departure from standard formal curriculum practice, which Klein would restore. Boër used a painted wooden model to teach pelvic anatomy. Except for a few brief periods, the incidence of death by puerperal fever over a period of 30 years was around 1 percent. It was .84 in 1823 when Boër resigned and Johann Klein was replaced him. Control of major faculty positions was in the hands of government ministers who assured that their appointees kept to the official line. As a result, Klein restored the standard curriculum: students learned to do obstetric exams by using cadavers. Constraints were relaxed on students and doctors' internal exams during labor and forceps deliveries. The mortality rate immediately soared to 7.45 percent.

* Ferdinand Schwarzmann von Hebra graduated in medicine in 1841 at the University. Like Semmelweis, Hebra was influenced by von Rokitansky. Hebra wrote one of the most influential books on dermatology, the Atlas der Hautkrankeiten (Atlas of skin diseases), with phenomenal illustrations by two of the leading medical illustrators, Anton Elfinger (1821–1864) and Carl Heizmann (1836–1896). In 1844, Hebra discovered the cause of scabies.

*Murphy. Professor of Obstetrics at London, He would write a long article (Dublin Quarterly Journal of Medical Science[24] 1857) in which he accepts the views expressed in Routh's notes. But Murphy also wrote that puerperal fever can have many other causes besides decaying organic matter, which Semmelweis had also advanced, and must not have included information about the two cases which, Semmelweis had proved, also caused puerperal fever. Dr. Murphy's lecture in behalf of Drs. Routh and

Semmelweis was published in 1849 in the *Medico-Chirugical Transactio.*

*Professor Kolletschka, more information on the important colleague of Semmelweis's can be found in *The Etiology, Concept, and Prophylaxis of Childbed Fever* by Ignaz Semmelweis, translated by K. Codell Carter: "Dear Kolletschka had his hands contaminated with decaying matter on countless occasions and he nevertheless remained healthy. Through a prick, resorption was possible; we know which disease was the consequence. The hands of the anatomist are often on contact with decaying corpses for hours at a time and he remains healthy. If the epidermis is removed by an injury, however, the disease is generated—this happened to Kolletschka. Obstetricians carry the matter on their hands for hours and even days without harming themselves. If this matter is brought into contact with the inner surface of the uterus, even for a moment, it is resorbed and childbed fever results.

*Chlorine was discovered in 1774 by Carl Wilhelm Scheele. He obtained it through the reaction of the mineral pyrolusite (manganese dioxide, MnO_2) with hydrochloric acid (HCl, then known as muriatic acid). Scheele thought the resulting gas contained oxygen. Sir Humphrey Davy proposed and confirmed chlorine to be an element in 1810, and he also named the element.

*contagion: The British obstetricians' belief that childbed fever was contagious would plague Semmelweis throughout his career. While in Vienna, he did not publish his beliefs in regard to the contagion theory, adding to his discreditation. He would wait 10 years to write:

"I regard childbed fever as a non-contagious disease because it cannot be conveyed from every patient with childbed fever to a healthy person, and because a healthy person can contract the disease from persons not suffering from childbed fever. Every victim of smallpox is capable of giving smallpox to healthy people. A healthy person can contract smallpox only from one who has smallpox. No one ever contracted smallpox form a person suffering from cancer of the uterus. This is not the case with childbed fever. If it takes a form in which no decaying matter is produced, then it cannot be communicated to a healthy person. However, given a form that produces decaying matter, i.e., septic endometritis, the disease is certainly communicable...Moreover, childbed fever may come from diseased states other than childbed fever, i.e., gangrenous erysipelas, carcinoma of the uterus, etc. A contagious disease is conveyed by the matter which is produced only by that particular disease, while childbed fever is conveyed by matter that is the product not only of childbed fever but also of the most heterogeneous diseases."

*Soon after Scanzoni and Seyfert's response, a student of Seyfert filed the following report. It is published in full to indicate the extent of the subterfuge that Semmelweis and his findings that Semmelweis was subject to. "Seyfert wanted to provide the clinical students with conclusive proof that the washings were entirely useless and that is was impossible to imagine that the infection of maternity patients with cadaverous matter resulted in the [diseased] puerperal state. One must realize that most of the examining students came directly from the morgue and so it was easy for cadaverous matter to be conveyed this way. In fact, in spite of the so-called washings, the disease, the disease did not become less frequent or less intense...But for me this was no proof against the views of Dr. Semmelweis, because I saw with my own eyes that there was usually nothing resembling a true washing of the hands. Usually, only the fingertips were dipped once into an opaque liquid that had served the same purpose for many days and that was itself completely saturated with harmful matter, Many of the gentlemen finally abandoned even this manipulation and used only ordinary water, often even without soap."

*Hugh Lenox Hodge was born in Philadelphia, June 27, 1796, the son of physician Hugh Lodge and Maria Blanchard. After an early education under Mr. Thompson at the Academy of the University of Pennsylvania and at boarding schools in New Jersey, young Hodge attended college at Princeton University along with his brother, Charles Hodge, the distinguished Presbyterian theologian. After his graduation from Princeton in 1814, Hodge began his study of medicine under Dr. Caspar Wistar. Hodge received his M.D. from the University of Pennsylvania in 1818. Immediately upon graduation, he took a voyage to India as a ship's surgeon. After his return in 1820, Hodge quickly became respected in the practice of anatomy and surgery, beginning practice as physician to the Southern Dispensary and the Philadelphia Dispensary. Hodge first taught at the University of Pennsylvania in 1821 as a substitute anatomy teacher for William E. Horner and then in 1823 as a surgery lecturer in Nathaniel Chapman's summer school. Unfortunately, failing eyesight led Hodge to abandon his career in surgery five years later. Although he was a founding editor of the *North American Medical and Surgical Journal* in 1826, Hodge shifted from surgery to obstetrics, resulting in a position as physician-in-charge of the lying-in department of Pennsylvania Hospital in 1832. In 1834 he replaced Dr. Thomas Chalkley James Professor of Obstetrics and the Diseases of

Women at the University of Pennsylvania. Hodge became influential in this new field, pioneering techniques and medical instruments that became widespread. Even after complete failure of his sight forced his resignation in 1863, he wrote (with the help of his sons) the widely acclaimed *Principles and Practices of Obstetrics* in 1864. Hodge remained an emeritus professor until his death on February 23, 1873. He and his wife Margaret E. Aspinwall had seven sons.

* After Skoda's lecture before the Imperial Academy of Vienna, Dr. Dr. Justus Liebig writes: "From this lecture it appears, incidentally, how little attention has been given to this large and practical discovery outside the Academy. Certainly, other causes of childbed fever will be identified. However, no unprejudiced person can doubt that the one identified so insightfully by Dr. Semmelweis at the maternity hospital in Vienna is among the causes. The universal cause of childbed fever is decaying matter." More than ten years later, Semmelweis wrote: "Liebig deleted this passage, so favorable to me, from the second edition of *Chemical Letters*, and I presumed to ask him why. With some trepidation that I might receive an answer expressing surprise at my naiveté, I also took the opportunity to ask Liebig for his opinion regarding the disinfective power of chlorine... I sought to learn of chemists about the

qualities of chlorine that brought Semmelweis to it as a disinfectant. Dr. Liebig is the first one to respond to me."Liebig's response to Semmelweis: "I am honored to reply to your letter that the omission of your observation regarding childbed fever from the new edition of my *Chemical Letters* was made not because I no longer recognize the importance of your experience. Rather it was because it is now so well and widely known that its retention in my book appeared to have not purpose; it did not relate directly to the subject matter....There is no doubt that chlorine possesses disinfective qualities."

*Ferenc Kölcsey's Anthem *Himnusz*

(Hungarian Lyrics):

Isten, áldd meg a magyart
Jó kedvvel, bőséggel,
  Nyújts feléje védő kart,
  Ha küzd ellenséggel;
  Bal sors akit régen tép,
  Hozz rá víg esztendőt,
Megbűnhődte már e nép
A múltat s jövendőt!

(English translation):

O, my God, the Magyar bless
With Thy plenty and good cheer!

With Thine aid his just cause press,
Where his foes to fight appear.

Fate, who for so long did'st frown,
Bring him happy times and ways;
Atoning sorrow hath weighed down
Sins of past and future days.

*Midwife's Oath. This incident is mentioned by Dr. Nuland and was mentioned also by Dr. Fleisher. Fleisher was not present at this meeting. The event was omitted from the minutes but circulated nevertheless. Dr. Fleisher mentions this event seven years after Semmelweis' death. He was not present so the event is hearsay, and it was not included in the meeting's minutes. Nevertheless, it circulated, just another opportunity, verified or not, to disparage Semmelweis and his work.

*William Sinclair: author of Semmelweis, His Life and His Doctrine: a Chapter in the History of

Medicine (Publications of the University of

Manchester, Medical Series, no. XI)

*The Commissioners of 1846 had declared that the foreign students were more dangerous to the patients because they made examinations in a rougher manner, but that was not the real reason. It was this: The foreigners come to Vienna to complete, in a few months, the medical studies which they have begun at some other university. They attend the pathological and medico-legal autopsies at the General Hospital. They take courses of pathological anatomy, of surgical, obstetrical and ophthalmological operations on the cadaver, and they attend the clinical work in medicine and surgery: in a word they do all they can in the time at their disposal, and they consequently find frequent occasions for rendering their hands unclean with putrid animal-organic material, and when they are practicing midwifery as well, simultaneously, it is easy to understand how they endanger the lives of lying-in women.

"On that account we have no more right to reproach them than to blame myself and others who, when we knew no better than examine parturient women with hands smelling of the dissecting-room, caused so many deaths."

*Johann Friedrich Osiander. His quote can be found in Hanover: Hahn, 1813, pp33, 46 [author's note].

* Dr. Nuland's work on the causes and author's investigation of the death of Semmelweis can be found in his book *The Doctors Plague,* pgs. 166-169

In view of the enormous interest in Semmelweis, new secrets about his life were still being discovered well into the 1970s. Nuland cites, for example, Georg Silló-Seidl, a Hungarian doctor, who, in 1977, found twelve pages of documents concerning him in the Vienna archives. They revealed for the first time details of Semmelweis's medical examination immediately before being sent to the asylum, the order sending him there, a medical record of his stay, the plan for his autopsy, and a final diagnosis. These papers describe his disturbed state of mind. According to the doctor who examined him, Semmelweis began to be indifferent to the family…. He sought opportunities to entertain himself elsewhere….[His drinking] exceeded the limits of moderation….His behavior became more unseemly….Those around him have noticed a heightened sexual excitement…. [H]e now established relationships with a prostitute. Once inside the asylum, he was excited, confused, and restless, speaking loudly, moving unpredictably, screaming occasionally, and entering periods of trembling frenzy. The final entries in the asylum's diary describe his lonely extinction: …he took off his clothes[, and] lay down on [the] floor.... He stutters more noticeably.... The right foot is dragged behind during his broad, uncertain walking.... He knows no one....Lower jaw hanging down somewhat...eyes glassy, half open.... Evening, death."

*Dr. Nuland considers unreliable Dr. Sillo-Seidl's discovery of papers obtained from the Viennese archive in 1977 concerning Semmelweis's behavior immediately before being sent off to the asylum, his final days there and his brutal death. Nuland rejects manic-depressive psychosis with paranoid features, which Dr. Irvine Loudon favors. Organic brain disease such as neuro-syphilis is suggested by Dr. Jones.

BIBLIOGRAPHY

The Life and Work of SEMMELWEIS – Louis Ferdinand Céline;(translated from the French by Robert Allerton Parker) New York-Howard Fertig, 1979.

Semmelweis – Louis Ferdinand Céline;(translated from the French by John Harman) Atlas Press, London, 2008

The Doctors' Plague: Germs, Childbed Fever, and the Strange Story of Ignác Semmelweis – Sherwin B. Nuland. W.W. Norton & Company 2003.

The Tragedy of Childbed Fever – Irvine Loudon, Oxford University Press – 2000

The Etiology, Concept and Prophylaxis of Childbed Fever – Ignaz Semmelweis,

Translated by K. Codell Carter – General Editors: William Coleman; David C. Lindberg; Ronald L. Numbers. The University of Wisconsin Press – 1983

The Lancet, Volume 383, Issue 9913, Pages 210 – 211, 18 January 2014, doi:10.1016/S0140-6736(14)60062-3

Carter and Carter, 1994 Carter KC, Carter BR. Childbed fever: a scientific biography of Ignaz Semmelweis. Westport, CT: Praeger, 1994.

Lerner, 2014 Lerner BH. The good doctor: a father, a son and the evolution of medical ethics. Boston: Beacon Press, 2014.

Lowenthal, 1986 Lowenthal D. The past is a foreign country. Cambridge: Cambridge University Press, 1986.

Nuland, 2004 Nuland SB. The doctors' plague: germs, childbed fever and the strange story of Ignác Semmelweis. New York: W. W. Norton, 2004.

Thompson, 1949 Thompson M. The cry and the covenant. New York: Doubleday, 1949.

Anthony Valerio is an author, book editor and university professor. He has published ten books of fiction & nonfiction, including *The Mediterranean Runs Through Brooklyn, Valentino and the Great Italians, Anita Garibaldi, a Biography; Dante in Love; Conversation with Johnny; BART, a Life of A. Bartlett Giamatti; The Little Sailor* and *Toni Cade Bambara's One Sicilian Night,* a memoir. His short stories have been published in the Paris Review. His work has been anthologized by Random House, William Morrow and The Viking Press. Mr. Valerio has taught at New York University, The City University of New York and Wesleyan University. He was a fiction judge on the PEN Prison Writing Committee. He is a member of The Authors League.

Anthony Valerio

www.ingramcontent.com/pod-product-compliance
Lightning Source LLC
Chambersburg PA
CBHW020150090426
42734CB00008B/771